6 - 5 · 78
Dr. Bauman
10^{30} AM.

New Theatre
In America

edited, with an introduction by

Edward Parone

 A Delta Book

A DELTA BOOK

Published by Dell Publishing Co., Inc.

750 Third Avenue, New York, N.Y. 10017

Typography by Barbara Luttringhaus

Library of Congress Catalog Card Number: 65–11851

Delta ® TM 755,118, Dell Publishing Co., Inc.

First printing—January, 1965

Fifth Printing

Manufactured in the United States of America

TABLE OF CONTENTS

Introduction

A POSTCARD FROM THE VOLCANO

Children picking up our bones
Will never know that these were once
As quick as foxes on the hill . . . . . .

And least will guess that with our bones
We left much more, left what still is
The look of things, left what we felt

At what we saw . . . .
And what we said of it became
A part of what it is.

       —Wallace Stevens
     "A Postcard from the Volcano"

I

Book titles are advertising. And advertising, like the art and
language it mimics, is a form of lie. And lies always have handy
rationalizations.

The New? American? Theatre?

Well, I don't suppose you could very well call a book *A
Trickle of One-Act Plays Written by American-born Playwrights
in the Last Couple of Years; Minus a Couple the Editor Wanted
to Include But the Agents and Publishers Could Not Agree on*

1

a Contract; and Omitting DIVERS OTHERS *Which Have Come to the Editor's Attention Too Late for Inclusion, etc. etc.*

But now that the financial success of *Tom Jones* has made the eighteenth century all right again, why not such a title?

Let it go . . . .

But what has happened that could make this book even thinkable in a paperback publication, when ten years ago most of the plays published were big Broadway hits—only?

Four things, at least, have happened:

Samuel Beckett, Jean Genet, Eugene Ionesco, Edward Albee.

Or:

The day literature returned to playwriting.

I do not want to go into comparing these four writers. BUT: I think that Beckett is a genius. (You may qualify this by adding "Playwriting, Dramatic or Theatre"). Genet is a very good playwright (with chronic second-act trouble), a marvellous *writer* (a better prose writer than practically anybody else alive). Ionesco has contributed a new form of mad humor, which, unfortunately, as time goes on is not being tempered with depth of feeling—tenderness *or* the kill.

Albee shot straight up out of American soil, with that peculiar American talent for catching on to what's happening at the moment it happens, and bringing to bear on it his own talent for digging around in the ruins of the civilized heart and coming up with a dramatic plan for what once was a man and a city—the ghosts of human dwellings. He shares this with Beckett and you must look, as they do, point-blank at the ruins, but deduce the building. It is hard and they do not take you by the hand. It's just bang on. And they both know how to *write*. Differently. But their plays are *constructions of language*.

It will be a long way to that dreary time when the "influence" of the three European playwrights on the theatre in general and the American theatre in particular will be weighed and sent aloft as another academic lead balloon. And, in the immortal words of Anky Larrabee, it will be a long green day in the land of the banana mashers before I do any such thing. But influence is obvious right now. The hundreds of plays that my colleagues and I have read in the past five years are mostly imitative of Beckett, Ionesco, Genet, and Albee. Most of them, as usual, are terrible; the arrival of the Europeans must have seemed like the answer to the prayers of those who don't know beans about writing or drama. The talented will, as usual, have to learn and unlearn their teachers. The technique and concept of Arthur Miller's *After the Fall*, although hinted at in *Death of a Salesman*, is freer and even more cinematic than any he has used before; and the audience does not bat an eye. Lillian Hellman, who has been breaking her well-made mold for years (usually with a Chekhovian chisel), became positively wild and woolly in her latest play. (And just so it doesn't come up later: yes, there *was*—or is—Thornton Wilder. And the plays of O'Casey and Synge *are* literature, too.)

But since this is a book of American plays, let's stick to that. I have no idea how much Albee was galvanized by the plays of the three Europeans and I wouldn't dream of asking any artist such a question. But it seems obvious, again, how many playwrights have been galvanized by Albee and his *success*.

Us Americans, we sure love new gadgets; but, sure as hell, we got to be *sold* on things. This literature play stuff is okay; but it's got to *sell*. If it sells, then that's all right.

Quite apart from any question of his artistic success or failure, Albee's box-office appeal has made several things all right for new American playwrights:

1. They are being taken somewhat more seriously by more dense theatrical managements. Their plays are at least being read by agents and producers—even if only out of a philosophy of "it *can* happen here."

2. One-act plays are not considered theatrical death. To be sure, no one has tried them on Broadway, although someone was *daring* enough to put on two previously-produced-in-London one-acters by Peter Shaffer, English of course. Daring David

Merrick, with a total of 36 productions, has produced only four plays written by American authors—one of these was first produced in England, one was a light comedy, one was an adaption of a novel, and the fourth was a revival.

3. Off-Broadway is no longer a dirty word to those who have been "on." It even seems possible that writers can alternate their work between the two places—although there is only one management that physically and philosophically really allows this; and although every—no, almost every—writer I know considers off-Broadway an annoyingly necessary step to that paradise in hell uptown where the biggest and only hits at this very moment (August, 1964) are: *Hello, Dolly* (a triumph of directorial genius); *Funny Girl* (an inferior version of what might have been a good movie biography starring Alice Faye); *Barefoot in the Park* (prurience brought to bear on married sex); *Any Wednesday* (prurience brought to bear on *un*married sex).

4. Playwrights are assuming (not re-suming) their place as the most important single element in the theatre. Stars can no longer carry bad or mediocre shows (e.g., Mary Martin, Jack Lemmon, Kirk Douglas, and the Actors' Studio production of *Strange Interlude*). Actors and producers are finding they are not necessarily writers (e.g., Actors' Studio production of *Marathon 33*; and *Herald Tribune* story describing actors rewriting an item called *Roar Like a Dove*). Directors no longer predominate. Elia Kazan and Joshua Logan, for instance, were nearly as famous as the playwrights and plays they directed. Alan Schneider, who directs both Beckett and Albee, is a comparative wallflower of a celebrity.

Us Americans, we like to exaggerate pretty much. We got a pretty kicky sense of humor going for us that way. We like to pile rewards on those we approve till they can't breathe. Of course we can strip them naked just as fast too. Only makes sense, doesn't it? One or the other? We are a long way from mastering, or even having, the technique of praise.

The "bitch" critics are furious with the theatre, and the good young critics who are on, or used to be on, or are sympathetic to, the *Village Voice* don't seem terribly at ease. The former cannot find—or rather, one cannot find in their writing—one thing that gives them pleasure, delight and/or enlightenment, except possibly obscure drag movies. The latter can find it in their hearts to heap awards on the Living Theatre and on a very valuable enterprise called the Judson Poet's Theatre, but pass in silence a director who does a brilliant job of staging one of the world's great plays.

But we need them. For what have we in the reviewers whom everybody reads and, usually, heeds? Let it be said once and for all: it is not *their* fault that people will decide, simply by reading their reviews, whether they will or will not see a play. Most newspaper drama reviewers exactly represent every kind of playgoer—except the most intelligent, the receptive, the sensitive. For instance, the reviewer for *the* important newspaper in New York, *mon dieu*, expressed astonishment, in his review of LeRoi Jones' *Dutchman*, that the Negro character in the play should feel violently about the white character! The same reviewer had earlier in the year professed equal astonishment in his review of *The Brig* that there was sadism in the Marine Corps! For instance the reviewers on the yellowest of tabloids—those papers compounded of movie-star scandal, inane photographs, and gossip columns of all kinds—could give Bowdler lessons in a show of outraged "decency" when confronted by *Who's Afraid of Virginia Woolf?* and *Dutchman*.

Us Americans, we're funny. We don't like anybody to tell us what to do or push us around. But a Broadway show *needs* unadulterated raves from at least four out of seven reviews to survive. An off-Broadway show might just as well shut down at once without raves from the *Times*, with assists from the *Post* and the *Tribune*.

But although everybody seems to be furious with the theatre (and this year everybody is *very* furious with the Lincoln Center

Repertory), everybody seems to be writing plays. And the number of promising scripts seems to be increasing.

Just as we are sometimes faced politically with a choice between something resembling Nazi Germany (or Stalinist Russia) and a rational human entente of free individuals, so in the theatre the tyranny of the sentimental and the mechanical persists against a louder and louder voice demanding equal time. This is supposed to be "that same old problem." It is not. Nazis *do* come to power and theatres *do* die.

Not six months after a beautiful failure like *Ballad of the Sad Cafe* and three months after the failure of Samuel Beckett's *Play*, a three-act domestic depressant opened on Broadway, where it was immediately ladled with giant dollops of syrupy praise like a caramel at Schrafft's. But the damned candy didn't *move* on the market! Apparently the crowd from that musical down the street had had enough dessert, and the off-Broadway type bunch couldn't possibly swallow it. What *then?* Why, there followed one of those curious theatrical rituals, a crusade—"sentimental binge" is a little better—to get that candy to those real kids, to *push* that stuff in every schoolyard in town. And did the crusade come off? Silly. (The most accurate description of this toothsticker came, of course, from one of its admirers. "Why, you know," he said, "the father said things in that play that I heard *my* old man say to me!")

But playwriting is respectable again. Almost nobody writes sensitive little short stories nowadays (besides, where would they be published?). Novels take too long (and what if you don't really catch *on* pornographically?). Everybody loves movies but you have to direct those yourself. Drama is possible. Poets, novelists, essayists, painters, and musicians all want to and do write plays. Very slowly literature is returning to drama; even poetry is coming back. For drama *is*, despite the years of brainwashing to the contrary, a form of literature. And "theatrical effectiveness" and beauty of form and language are *not* mutually exclusive concepts. Drama *is* language. Poetry (even lyric poetry) *is* dramatic. The stage is the place for *words*, not for plangent silences between actors (*vide Anthony and Cleopatra;* then *cf. A Hatful of Rain.* And Chekhov *not* to the contrary).

Now us Americans, we don't like to support things out of public funds—subsidize, don't you know. It kind of hits us sideways. Involves value judgments, don't you know. Might even be C——ist. So we don't got no subsidized theatre. What we *got,* we got Foundations. Like the Ford Foundation. The Rockefeller Foundation. The Guggenheim Foundation.

Now the Ford Foundation, they *tried* giving awards to playwrights, but that didn't work too hot, didn't come up with any *winners* the first year. So they give awards to poets and novelists to go sit in theatres here and there and learn how to write plays. Only they don't seem to give any to poets and novelists with any talent for and/or interest in the theatre. And I personally know two good poets who *have* a talent for and interest in the theatre. But they don't have Ford grants.

Now the Rockefeller Foundation, *they* tried giving awards to playwrights. And they sent them out to a big Midwestern university to put on their plays. But the university, they didn't think those particular plays should be put on in front of *audiences.*

Now the Guggenheim Foundation, they *never* give awards to playwrights. What's playwrights?

Now us Americans, we like to know the worth of a thing. Does it give good value for your money? Is it made good? Will it *last?*

Will *what* last? In this most transient country and culture in a peripatetic world?

II

Any fool can plainly see that this introduction is not conspicuous for its balanced, academic argument. It is not intended to. I am not interested in point-killing debate, but only in the emotional *sense* of what is going. It is well and necessary and right to argue points of law and use them (with the risk of abusing them) for the protection of human rights. But no one ever *talks* any more about the precepts on which those laws are based—least of all a politician (in whatever field). No one starts out by saying something that apparently is no longer evident to many people: that it is *morally wrong* to deprive any person of any human right for any reason whatsoever.

The above will strike some as "political"—ha—and what has it got to do with the theatre? It has this to do with it: the theatre and all art business in this country are operating in the same way: indifference masked as srength or tough-mindedness; cynicism masked as central intelligence; and plain old lying. Almost no producer in New York is even tokenly interested in producing or even fostering American drama that bears remotely on truth of any kind. Let alone any variations on technique or form or style. Quite apart from the dim-witted foundations, quite apart from the absurdly rich television machine and the powerful movie business, there are three or four producers who have grown rich beyond the dreams of avarice in the theatre. And not one of them puts one damn cent back into it in any way except the manufacture of more and bigger and more sickening caramels. Almost nowhere does one feel, let alone hear, a basic precept: the theatre is for the enlightenment and enrichment of the human condition. Not the degradation of it, with default of "product" as the usual excuse.

And it has this to do with it: obviously the political climate—the human climate—of this country is directly related to its art and specifically to the plays that are written and/or produced. We are more and more a country of spoiled children. No one is encouraged to grow up. Who is to do the encouraging? Other children? Even some of our best artists suffer from naiveté more than any other single failing. And everything that is wrong with our art and artists—naiveté, impatience, false shock, prurience, superficiality, timidity of reach, flight from the reality of ugliness as well as beauty—all of this is a direct result of and a di-

rect reflection of who and what we are. And ponderous foundations, more theatres, cheaper union rates, supervised ticket
scalping do no more good than the mayor's sending in more
cops to solve violence on subways, riots in Harlem, and teen-age
drunken driving.

We do not grow up or grow old. We get hard-boiled, dry up
and blow away. Children? we say. Then why don't they grow
up if they really want to? (Rather reminds one of the recently
proposed argument: Poor people? Well, why don't they get
rich?) This is no country for the old.

There are no doubt "statistics" to prove—and it certainly
seems to be true—that more books are being bought, more rec-
ords being sold, more concerts attended, more paintings bought,
etc., etc., than ever before. It should also be obvious by now
that promiscuity prepares you only for more promiscuity. It
does not prepare you for love. Or understanding. Or knowledge.

Is this too much weight or importance to give to the art of
the theatre? I don't think so. And it is not even that everybody
who writes seriously for the theatre is "purely" motivated or
"purely" telling the truth. They are capable of being, and sometimes are, fools—*trying not to be liars.* It is not very remarkable
that some people still want to become artists; it is simply miracu-
lous that there are any at all. Just try, for instance, being
Tennessee Williams, Arthur Miller, Lillian Hellman, or Edward Albee up against the bitch critics. If you think box-office
failure is hair-raising, just try artistic failure. Not only does it
jeopardize the artist's future; it jeopardizes his *past.*

We honor what shows us off, what flatters us, what idealizes
us, what makes us money, what puts us to sleep, what corrupts
and what sickens. We do not honor art or artists. This is no
country for that.

Yet here we are faced with this burst of drama.

Perhaps the only country that should be touched on for pur-
poses of comparison should be England. According to a book
called *Anger and After* (an examination and a record of English drama since the emergence of John Osborne) and according

to an English play agent who specializes in new young dramatists, the theatrical explosion that everyone expected in England
has not taken place. Joan Littlewood excites everyone a lot, but
she is a *director*. The Royal Court seems to have lost its leading
lights to the movies and the West End. Harold Pinter, who
seems to have become the leading English playwright, last
wrote a play in 1959; others of his that we have seen in this
country as plays were written originally for television. The literary agent says that they (the English) are panting for new
American playwrights. Nothing like the quantity and quality of
new American plays is being written in England.

Oh, that's all right, dears. Our madhouse is bigger. And not
only do we still have with us a lot of uppity (and angry) white
boys, but we have that enormous Negro heart that has never,
never really, been heard from.

III

Not so incidentally, this book might have been subtitled: *A
Collection of Plays Mostly Discovered and Produced by Theater
1965*. (This is a production company formed by Richard Barr,
Clinton Wilder, and Edward Albee). With two exceptions they
were all produced at their Cherry Lane Theatre or in their Playwrights Unit Workshop.

There are exceptions to the general Broaday rule to ignore
the new and the newcomer. Three of these exceptions are
specifically geared for the playwright. The New Dramatists
Committee, the oldest of the exceptions, is also the most con-
ventional. It was formed by some of the established Broadway
producers, directors, and agents. The members are lectured to;
they have readings of their plays; they are assigned as observers
to Broadway plays and musicals throughout production. The
Committee is supported by various professionals in the theatre;
it also has foundation money. Its alumni include Robert Ander-
son, William Inge, Joseph Masteroff, and Muriel Resnik.

The Actors' Studio formed its Playwrights Unit a few years ago. Plays or scenes from plays by the members are performed usually, though not always, by Studio actors. The unit is run by a committee; meetings are held. Discussions take place after the performances. The unit is supported by the Studio, with foundation money for a specified number of projects. But the Studio, it seems from my observation, is in theory and practice an *actors'* studio, not a playwrights' or even directors'. And perhaps the following true story may be pertinent, though it may not be typical. A young actress, a member of the Studio, came to read for the part of the girl in LeRoi Jones' *Dutchman*. She mounted the stage and, riffling the script in her hands and looking somewhere between the playwright and the director, said, "Uh, you don't care if I don't bother to use the lines, do you?"

The Theater 1965 Playwrights Unit was formed in 1964. Playwrights were chosen from a list of "promising" writers who had submitted plays to the producers over a period of a few years. No meetings are held except at the beginning and end of the season. Fully rehearsed and staged plays or scenes are given in workshop production nearly every week. The choice of director, actor, audience, and discussion is left entirely to the playwright. The Unit is supported by the producers themselves; there is no foundation money. The unique and valuable distinction of this particular unit—connected as it is with a regularly producing company—is that it seems to have given more writers everywhere the assurance that there really exists a place—perhaps three places—where their work can be seen. The theatre, then, this theatre, is *accessible*.

IV

It is unfair for the few plays and playwrights in this book to have to bear the burden of indicating the extent and variety of what is happening to drama in America today (and the foregoing remarks probably doesn't make it any easier for them). Perhaps a couple of hundred plays, both good and bad, would have to be included, and even more than one play by these seven men, for it to be fair.

In any case, the plays here were not chosen to "represent" any particular kind of writing or technique or subject. Actually it was the playwrights who were selected, not the plays. (Adrienne Kennedy and Terrance McNally should be included in this book, but regrettably it was not possible. Others who have emerged since the book was compiled will be included in a possible second volume.)

Most of these plays are by now early works; five of them have been produced in workshops and/or off-Broadway; five of them are published here for the first time. All the writers are currently at work on new plays.

For me to write criticism of these plays would be like inviting people to a party and picking their behavior apart. They are here obviously because we feel they have talent; that they are *writers,* not theatrical technicians constructed for the Great White Way; that they have and will have something to say.

To say anything more than that would make it appear to defend them—which they don't need. Since they themselves have put their work out into the world, they apparently are willing to take risks. It is always extraordinary these days when anyone is willing to do that.

V

DR. ARBUTHNOT: And what kind of a lin play is it?
"A Darlin' Play . . ." Atkinson, *Times*
DR. ARBUTHNOT: And what kind of a damned musical was it you've seen in years?
"Best damned musical I've seen in years." Kerr, *Tribune*
DR. ARBUTHNOT: And how long should it almost run for?
"Should run almost forever." Chapman, *News*

DR. ARBUTHNOT: What kind of ment seems to be going on in the American theatre today?

CLICHÉ EXPERT: A fer-ment seems to be going on in the American theatre today.

DR. ARBUTHNOT: What kind of ment with the status quo do our playwrights seem to be expressing?

CLICHÉ EXPERT: Our writers seem to be expressing discontent-ment with the status quo.

DR. ARBUTHNOT: What kind of ment may they become bright lights in the theatrical of?

CLICHÉ EXPERT: May become bright lights in the theatrical firma-ment.

Perhaps nothing is more damning proof of the statements, assertions, and generalizations made in this essay than its own ingenuousness and the sad fact that someone felt that anything so obvious needed to be said.

There is, then, a short Anglo-Saxon word fitting enough to end and comment on this essay. There is also a more literary one from e. e. cummings: "A politician is an arse upon which everyone has sat except a man."

—*Edward Parone*
New York City
August, 1964

Mrs. Dally Has A Lover

William Hanley

FOR PANOS

SCENE: A *kitchen, New York City, January.*

First presented at The Cherry Lane Theatre, New York,
October 1, 1962.

CAST

Mrs. Dally .... Estelle Parsons
Frankie .... Robert Drivas

Directed by Richard Altman

The kitchen of a railroad apartment, old and shabby, but apparently as orderly and clean as circumstances permit. At the left are windows, two of them, closed. Up-center, leading to the back hallway: a service door, on the knob of which is hung a man's coat. To the left of this door: the door to the bathroom. There is a table, with chairs, in the center of the room. At the right, a doorway hung with a drape: if one were to throw a stone through this door it would pass through a small bedroom, a somewhat larger bedroom, the living room and the living-room window, and land in a street lined with mutilated brownstone and ash-cans.

After a moment, MRS. DALLY *enters from the right, slippers slapping, tying the cord of a thin, green housedress. She is in her late thirties, red-haired and, all things considered, in good condition.*

She starts toward the stove but becomes tangled in a man's white shirt, lying on the floor, which she picks up and hangs carefully over the back of a chair. She ignites the gas under the coffeepot and, humming "Beautiful Dreamer," disappears into the bathroom.

As the door closes behind her, FRANKIE *appears at the bedroom door. He is an ordinary-looking boy of eighteen, and is shirtless.*

FRANKIE: What happened to my—? [*He sees the shirt, takes it from the chair and returns with it to the bedroom.* MRS. DALLY *emerges from the bathroom, a hairbrush in her hand. She proceeds to set the table with cups, milk and sugar, brushing her hair with her free hand.* FRANKIE *appears at the door, holding open his shirt.*] Hey, look.

MRS. DALLY: What?

17

FRANKIE: The buttons. There's no buttons. [*She approaches and inspects the shirt.*]

MRS. DALLY: Did *I* do that?

FRANKIE: Well, *I* didn't. [*She looks at him with a peculiar combination of embarrassment and coyness.*]

MRS. DALLY: I'm sorry.

FRANKIE [*Embarrassed, but for her, not himself*]: Jeez!

MRS. DALLY: They must be around, I'll sew 'em back on. [*She scans the floor with her eyes and begins to retrieve the buttons;* FRANKIE *finds one, but is not applying himself.*] How many are there?

FRANKIE [*Counting the holes*]: Six.

MRS. DALLY: You want some coffee? I'm makin' some.

FRANKIE: Okay.

MRS. DALLY: How many you got? I got four.

FRANKIE: One.

MRS. DALLY [*On her knees, peering*]: One more.

FRANKIE: There it is.

MRS. DALLY: Where?

FRANKIE: Right there, by your foot.

MRS. DALLY: You got good eyes, too. [*She gets to her feet.*] So you want some coffee?

FRANKIE: Yeah, sure.

MRS. DALLY: I mean, you ain't in a hurry or anything.

FRANKIE: No, I ain't in a hurry. [*He sits while she takes the coffeepot from the stove and places it on the table.*]

MRS. DALLY: I gotta get a needle and thread. [*She goes out; pause.* FRANKIE *regards the buttonless shirt with a shake of his head, then pours his coffee.* MRS. DALLY *returns from the bedroom with a sewing box, a former candy tin, and stops at the door, gazing at* FRANKIE, *whose back is to her; she approaches and places her hands on his shoulders.*] You have to take it off, sweetheart. [*He wriggles out of the shirt; she takes it and kisses his bare shoulder. As she makes her way around the table to sit opposite him,* FRANKIE *absently rubs the kiss from his shoulder, an action she does not see.*]

FRANKIE: Lucky I don't have buttons on my pants.

MRS. DALLY: Fresh. [*She pours her coffee.*] Coffee all right?

FRANKIE: Yeah, great.

[*It becomes evident now that* FRANKIE *has a consistent tendency to speak to her out of the corner of his eye.*]

MRS. DALLY: You want something to eat, a sandwich or something?

FRANKIE: No, I ain't hungry.

MRS. DALLY: Not for sandwiches, anyway.

FRANKIE [*He heard; but, smiling self-consciously*]:   What?

MRS. DALLY: I said, "Not for sandwiches, anyway."

FRANKIE: I ain't the only one.

[*Pause*]

MRS. DALLY: You know, I was almost raped once when I was sixteen?

FRANKIE: Yeah? What happened?

MRS. DALLY: I wasn't.

FRANKIE: I know, but I mean, how come?

MRS. DALLY: I told the guy I had syphilis.

[FRANKIE *starts almost imperceptibly.*]

FRANKIE: You did?

MRS. DALLY: Yeah.

FRANKIE: You had the syph when you was sixteen?

MRS. DALLY: No! I didn't *have* syphilis! I thought you meant did I *tell* him I had it.

FRANKIE: No, I meant did you have it.

MRS. DALLY: No, I didn't really have it, I only told him I had it.

FRANKIE: He believed you?

MRS. DALLY: He didn't wanta take a chance on not.

FRANKIE: That was pretty smart.

MRS. DALLY: Well, there's certain times when a girl has to think fast—like in rape. I mean, you lose your head and you're outa luck. So I just told him I had syphilis. He says, "You're lyin'!" I said, "So go ahead then and find out."

FRANKIE: He didn't wanta take the chance though, huh?

MRS. DALLY: What the hell, would you?

FRANKIE: No, I guess not.

MRS. DALLY: He beat the hell outa me, but he didn't rape me. Well, what the hell . . .

FRANKIE: I'll hafta remember that next time somebody tries to rape me.

MRS. DALLY: Fresh.

FRANKIE [*Debonairly*]:   Well, I mean, uh . . .

MRS. DALLY: Frankie . . . you got a lotta girl friends?

FRANKIE: Ohh, twenty or thirty, somethin' like that.

MRS. DALLY: No, I mean it.

FRANKIE: Well, you know, a couple, yeah. Why?

MRS. DALLY: I was just wondering. Listen, get a load of me letting you sit there without a shirt or nothin'. I better get you something to put on before you catch a cold.

FRANKIE: No, that's okay. [*She is already on her way.*] Look, I don't need . . . [*She has gone into the bedroom.*]

MRS. DALLY [*Off-stage*]:   I got just the thing. [*She reenters carrying a violently-colored man's cardigan sweater.*] It's never even been worn. It's *his*, you know? I bought it for him last Christmas, but he wouldn't even wear it. I told him they're very popular now, everybody wears 'em, but he wouldn't. He's got no class, you know? No class. The brute. Here, put it on. [*He does, and is lost in it.*]

FRANKIE: It's a little big.

MRS. DALLY: The brute. . . . Well, it looks very nice on you, I mean, if it was a little smaller.

FRANKIE: Yeah, well it's a little too big.

MRS. DALLY: I hate to see a beautiful garment like that going to waste. He says he couldn't wear the thing. The color, you know? So I said he could wear it working. He says, can I imagine him wearing a thing like that driving a cab. I said, he'd be the classiest-looking cab driver in the whole city. But no, not him. Then I said, well, he could wear it around the house, at least I'd get to see it. He says, "Suppose somebody comes to the door." Then he says I should change it and get another color, *then* maybe he'd wear it.

FRANKIE [*Advisedly*]:   That woulda been a good idea.

MRS. DALLY: That's the color I bought him, that's the color he's got. . . . I mean, don't you think that's a nice color?

FRANKIE: Yeah, it's very nice.

MRS. DALLY: Sure.

FRANKIE: A little . . . bright, maybe. For a guy.

MRS. DALLY: Yeah, well, I thought it might brighten up his personality a little. Not him. [*Pause, she sews.*]

FRANKIE: How come you asked me before if I had any girl friends?

MRS. DALLY: Oh, I was just curious.

FRANKIE: Oh.

MRS. DALLY: Curiosity killed the cat, hah?

FRANKIE: No, but I mean, d'ya think I didn't have any girl friends, or something?

MRS. DALLY: No, I didn't think that.

FRANKIE: I mean, I ain't Marlon Brando, okay, but I do all right.

MRS. DALLY: What I meant was, do you have girl friends that're . . . nice to you.

FRANKIE: Sure they're nice to me.

MRS. DALLY [*Carefully*]:   I mean are they as nice as me?

FRANKIE: What do you mean, do they put out?

[*The expression gives her pause.*]

MRS. DALLY: Yes, I suppose that's what I meant.

FRANKIE: Nah, they're just kids. Well, one maybe. Sometimes. On the roof, you know? Why'd you wanta know?

MRS. DALLY: I just wondered.

FRANKIE: Well, they're just kids.

[*Pause.*]

MRS. DALLY: Frankie . . . do you like me?

FRANKIE: Sure I like you.

MRS. DALLY: No, but I mean, do you *really* like me. I mean, do you . . . think about me?

FRANKIE: Well sure I think about you. I'm thinking about you right now.

MRS. DALLY: But when you're not here, when you're some-place else, do you think about me then?

FRANKIE: Sure.

MRS. DALLY: What do you think?

FRANKIE: What?

MRS. DALLY: What do you think? Like when you're walking down the street, and you think about me, what do you think?

FRANKIE: Well, I don't know, I never thought about it. I mean, about what I think. You just think, don't ya? How can you think about what you think?

MRS. DALLY: Do you think I'm pretty?

FRANKIE: Sure.

MRS. DALLY: Do you think . . . I have a nice figure.

FRANKIE: Hell, yes!

MRS. DALLY: Actually, I'm in pretty good shape, all things considered. I mean, for a woman my age, I'm in pretty good condition. [Pause.] Maybe I'm nuts.

FRANKIE: Why? [She only shakes her head.] Listen, if you really want to know something, I think you're . . . very beautiful.

MRS. DALLY: Really?

FRANKIE: Sure.

MRS. DALLY: It's very nice of you to say so, Frankie.

FRANKIE: Don't mention it. I figured you knew it, I didn't have to say it.

MRS. DALLY: No, you could say it once in a while, that would be all right.

FRANKIE: Like my old man says.

MRS. DALLY: What?

FRANKIE: Women're always fishin' for compliments.

MRS. DALLY [Wryly]: Yeah, we're a real nuisance.

FRANKIE: So my mother says if she got one once in a while she wouldn't hafta fish for it.

MRS. DALLY [*Nodding affirmation*]:   I always liked your mother.

FRANKIE: You know my mother?

MRS. DALLY: Just to say hello to in the A&P.

FRANKIE: Oh. I thought you meant you knew her. That would be funny.

[*Her pained glance escapes him.*]

MRS. DALLY: She's nice, your mother.

FRANKIE: I don't remember when you moved in here, I must've been a kid, just.

MRS. DALLY: A fresh kid—the same as you are now.

[*There are certain questions that, asked at certain moments, sound like accusations.* FRANKIE *asks one now.*]

FRANKIE: How old are you, anyway?

MRS. DALLY: None of your beeswax.

FRANKIE: No, I mean it, how old?

MRS. DALLY: Sweetheart, you should never ask a woman how old she is—unless, maybe, she's under twenty or over seventy.

FRANKIE: Why?

MRS. DALLY: Because everyplace in between, it's touch and go all the way.

FRANKIE: How come women act so funny about how old they are? The same with my mother. I asked her once how old she is, she wouldn't tell me. The only reason I know is I saw it on my birth certificate. How come?

MRS. DALLY: 'Cause there's a rumor we depreciate with age —like we were automobiles or something. A couple of dents in the fender, a scratch here and there and you start looking around for a new model. [*She hesitates a moment, then adds:*] I'm thirty-five.

FRANKIE: Thirty-five. I got me a real woman.

MRS. DALLY: You have, sweetheart. But not because I'm thirty-five.

FRANKIE: Well, you know what I mean: age, experience.

MRS. DALLY: Yeah, I know what you mean.

FRANKIE: I figured you were younger than that, even.

MRS. DALLY: Did you? Why?

FRANKIE: My mother's thirty-six and she looks a lot older than you. But that's probably because of all the kids. Kids make a woman get older a lot faster, right? I mean, havin' them.

MRS. DALLY: Who told you that?

FRANKIE: I don't know, I read it somewhere, I think. [*Then asks another of those questions:*] How come you don't have any kids?

MRS. DALLY: Boy! What're you, writing a book?

FRANKIE: I just wondered.

[*Pause.*]

MRS. DALLY: I had a kid.

FRANKIE: Where is it?

MRS. DALLY: He wasn't an "it," sweetheart. He was a boy. . . . He died.

FRANKIE [*Moved*]:   Oh . . . that's too bad.

MRS. DALLY: He was three years old. He drowned.

FRANKIE: That's really a shame. . . . You shoulda had another one, maybe.

MRS. DALLY: Well, it was kinda like when I lost one, I lost them all. When he came out of me, he brought a lot of my insides with him, you see? There were a lotta technical words for it but that's what it came down to, I couldn't have any more.

FRANKIE: Yeah. . . . That's really a shame.

MRS. DALLY: Yeah. [*She rises abruptly, takes the coffeepot to the stove, lights the gas beneath it.*] His name was Alan.

FRANKIE: What?

MRS. DALLY: The kid. His name was Alan. It's a nice name, don't you think?

FRANKIE: Yeah. Very nice.

MRS. DALLY: After Alan Ladd. You ever see *The Glass Key?*

FRANKIE: The what?

MRS. DALLY: The movie. *The Glass Key.* With Alan Ladd?

[*He shakes his head, somewhat confused.*] He was real great. You know, with the raincoat and all. 'Course, *he* didn't know I named the kid after Alan Ladd.

FRANKIE: Alan Ladd didn't?

MRS. DALLY: No, silly! *Him.* The brute.

FRANKIE: Oh.

MRS. DALLY: I just told him I wanted to call him Alan. He wanted to name the kid after himself. Could you believe it? I mean, you know what his name is?

FRANKIE: Sam.

MRS. DALLY: Well, everybody calls him Sam, that's the way he writes his name and all, but you know what his *real* name is? *Samson.* Can y'imagine anyone with a name like that? I mean, *Samson.* He's Samson, all right, but with a haircut, if you know what I mean. [*She turns off the gas, returns to the table with the coffeepot, fills her own cup, then* FRANKIE'S.] You know what I mean?

FRANKIE [*Smiling*]:   Yeah, I think so.

MRS. DALLY: Not that there aren't reasons, of course. I mean, for instance, one time I found out he was—you ready for this? —he was going around with two other dames. Two. Naturally, by the time he got around to me he was all worn out. [*She gazes at* FRANKIE *a moment, then puts her hand in his hair.*] You're so young and strong, Frankie. [*He touches her tentatively; they are like this for a moment; then she moves away, placing the coffeepot on the table.*] You wanta see a picture of him? My kid?

FRANKIE: Sure.

MRS. DALLY: Wait a sec. [*She goes quickly into the bedroom. A drawer is heard to open and close, and she returns with a large, thick photograph album.*]

FRANKIE: A picture.

MRS. DALLY: Don't worry, it ain't as much as it looks. [*She places the album on the table, opens it to the first page; then she closes it again, pointing out to him the name on the cover in large letters.*] Alan. Nice, huh? Fourteen-carat gold leaf.

[*She reopens the album.*] I don't have any baby pictures of
him, these were all when he was three years old. I had some
baby pictures of him, but I lost them, and I gave some of
them to my in-laws and *they* lost them, so then I got the idea
of this album, so these are all when he was three years old.
What about that kid, huh?

FRANKIE: Yeah. . . . You were really something, too.

MRS. DALLY: Yeah, but what *about* that kid, huh?

FRANKIE: Cute. [*He turns the page: it is blank. He turns another, riffles through the album; all blank.*] That's all you got?
One page?

[*Pause; she gazes vaguely at the album. When she speaks, the
answer is obvious yet seems to surprise her.*]

MRS. DALLY: He died. [*Pause; she takes the album from him,
sits again and places the album on the table before her.*] Stupid, huh? So thick. I figured on about twenty years. . . .
What're you gonna do, Frankie?

FRANKIE: Huh?

MRS. DALLY: What're you gonna do? I mean, what're you
gonna do in your *life*?

FRANKIE: Ohh, I don't know. I ain't decided.

MRS. DALLY: Working nights in a factory ain't any way to
spend a life, Frankie.

FRANKIE: I know. It was just the first job I took. After I
graduated high school. I ain't gonna spend my *life* there,
don't worry. One thing I'm gonna do is make a lotta
money.

MRS. DALLY: Why?

FRANKIE [*With a shrug: obviously*]:   Money talks.

MRS. DALLY: Yeah? What does it say? . . . You know what
I woulda done if I was a man?

FRANKIE: What?

MRS. DALLY: I woulda built bridges.

FRANKIE: Bridges! What kinda bridges?

MRS. DALLY: Bridges. Across rivers.

FRANKIE: What the hell for?

MRS. DALLY: Oh, I love bridges. Ever since I was a little girl I loved bridges. There's somethin' about 'em.

FRANKIE: What?

MRS. DALLY: Oh, I don't know, it's like . . . You ever stood in the middle of a bridge?

FRANKIE: I went *over* a lotta bridges.

MRS. DALLY: But've you ever stood in the middle of one?

FRANKIE: No.

MRS. DALLY: Well, you stand in the middle of a bridge, it's like . . . it's like a long pair of arms holding everything together. You know what I mean? When I was a kid, you know, we lived in Washington Heights, I could see the George Washington Bridge from my bedroom window. And you know what I always thought? This was when I was a little kid, I mean, but you know what I thought?

FRANKIE: What?

MRS. DALLY: I thought if the bridge wasn't there, New Jersey would just . . . float away.

FRANKIE: That's pretty funny.

MRS. DALLY: Yeah, well, when you're a kid, you know . . .

FRANKIE: Actually, I don't think it'd be missed.

MRS. DALLY [*She is absorbed and hasn't heard his remark*]: Oh, yeah, if I woulda been a man I'd've built bridges.

FRANKIE: Well, I'm just as glad.

MRS. DALLY: About what?

FRANKIE: That you wasn't a man.

MRS. DALLY: Yeah, it's had its compensations. *He* would've built bridges. [*She jabs the album with her finger.*] I started savin' up for it when he was three months old. But no, not *him*, *his* kid hasta learn how to swim. Three years old and he hasta learn how to swim just because his old man was a big swimming champion in high school. Three years old. He'll sink or swim, he says, he'll sink or swim. Well . . . he sank.

FRANKIE: Jesus! You mean he let him *drown*?

MRS. DALLY: No, no, no. But he wasn't watching. I mean, you don't turn your back on a three-year-old kid at a swimming pool. You just don't *do* a thing like that. But I knew what happened. I *told* him I knew and he finally admitted it. Talking to some girl. He could never keep his eyes off the girls, even after we were married. The funny thing is, if the pool wasn't so crowded, somebody probably woulda seen the kid. But there were so many people, you know how crowded those public pools get in the summer . . . no one even noticed. I mean, he drowned with all those people around. . . .

FRANKIE: Yeah.

MRS. DALLY: I guess I shouldn't've blamed him but I always did. It's a terrible thing, Frankie, to know you should forgive and not be able to. . . . He even cried when he admitted how it happened. I *told* him I knew and he finally admitted he was talking to this girl and then he started crying and then he started hitting me. *Him* hitting *me*. He still does, now and again. . . . I'd rather be hit by a truck than a man. . . . So the money I was saving up for the kid to be an engineer, it went for his funeral.

[*Pause.*]

FRANKIE: I always wondered why you didn't have any kids. [*Pause.*] If you wanted, maybe I could give you one of my kid sisters. [*She smiles, sadly amused.*] Listen, I don't think my mother'd mind so much, either. She's always sayin' how they're drivin' her nuts.

MRS. DALLY: I could think of some worse ways to go nuts.

FRANKIE: Yeah, well, she's always sayin' how if we weren't Catholics I wouldn't even have any brothers and sisters.

MRS. DALLY: She don't say that in front of the kids, does she?

FRANKIE: Sure. I mean, that's why she says it, to let 'em know where they stand, you know?

MRS. DALLY: She shouldn't say that in front of the kids. Look, let's stop talking about your mother, okay?

FRANKIE: Sure.

MRS. DALLY: I'm beginnin' to feel like your aunt or something.

FRANKIE [*Significantly*]:   You're not my aunt.

MRS. DALLY: A good thing too. That's all I'd need; it ain't bad enough. [*She resumes sewing.*]

FRANKIE: What do you mean?

MRS. DALLY: What?

FRANKIE: What do you mean, it ain't bad enough?

MRS. DALLY: I mean you and me.

FRANKIE: What's bad about it?

MRS. DALLY [*After regarding him for a moment*]: You're a funny kid, Frankie.

FRANKIE: A laugh a minute, but what's bad about it?

MRS. DALLY: Your age, sweetheart. My age. It's supposed to be unnatural.

FRANKIE: I don't care what it's supposed to be.

MRS. DALLY: No?

FRANKIE: No. Do you?

MRS. DALLY [*After a moment*]: No, I don't care about it.

FRANKIE: I mean, it ain't like we're married. That'd be different.

MRS. DALLY [*Cautiously*]: Would it?

FRANKIE: I mean, then it would maybe look kinda funny.

MRS. DALLY [*With mounting tension*]: Who said anything about married?

FRANKIE: Nobody. I was only sayin'.

MRS. DALLY: I already got a husband.

FRANKIE: I know. I was only sayin'. [*She works intensely at the button.*] You sore at me or something?

MRS. DALLY: No. OW! *Now,* look what you made me do!

FRANKIE: Me!

MRS. DALLY [*Fiercely*]: Well, if you unbuttoned your own shirt I wouldn't hafta—[*She breaks off, hearing herself; they look at each other for a moment and both smile.*]

FRANKIE: D'ya hurt yourself?

MR. DALLY: I think I'm gonna live. [FRANKIE *rises, takes her hand in his and kisses the wounded finger; it is an awkward gesture for him, but a genuine one and it moves her.*] Frankie, you got a few surprises in you, I think.

FRANKIE [*Escaping; fingering the sweater*]:   I feel like an A-rab in a tent.

MRS. DALLY: You're an Italian in a sweater. I'll be done with this in a minute. That's a lotta buttons, six buttons.

FRANKIE: Maybe I should get a zipper put on it.

MRS. DALLY: Fresh. [FRANKIE *is at the window, looking into the yard. Their backs are to each other now. A moment of silence; he speaks without turning.*]

FRANKIE: You don't . . . you don't like your husband, do you?

MRS. DALLY [*After a moment's hesitation*]:   Whatta you mean?

FRANKIE: Well, you know, I mean . . . you don't love him.

MRS. DALLY: Why didn't you say so?

FRANKIE: What?

MRS. DALLY: Love. [*He turns back to the window, staring intently into the yard without answering.*] You don't know how to use that word yet, do you, sweetheart. Well, you'll learn. [*She turns to look at him, then resumes sewing.*] What're you doing, thinking about jumping?

FRANKIE: No, I was looking at the kids. My sisters. They're playin' in the back yard.

MRS. DALLY: What're they, twins or what?

FRANKIE: Yeah.

MRS. DALLY: Pretty. [*She adds:*] Don't let 'em see you.

FRANKIE: Why not?

MR. DALLY: They might wonder what you're doing in the wrong apartment, that's why not.

FRANKIE: They can't see me. Crazy kids. They got this nutty game they play now, you know? I mean, they play it and the rest of us gotta listen to it, my brother and me and my mother and father. We all hafta sit down, they stand on the kitchen table and they do this thing. They call it "A Recital of Interesting Noises." They take turns making these nutty noises, you should hear some of the noises they come out with. Then the rest of us gotta vote and say which one made the most interesting noise. Nutty kids.

MRS. DALLY [*Ruefully; as opposed to adults*]:   *Kids* got the best games.

FRANKIE: They got the nuttiest ones.

MRS. DALLY: I'll tell you something, I've heard a *lotta* people playin' that game, only they weren't kids and they didn't call it that.

FRANKIE: What'd they call it?

MRS. DALLY: Talking.

FRANKIE [*Dodging quickly away from the window*]:   Oh, oh.

MRS. DALLY: What?

FRANKIE: They saw me, I think. . . . Yeah, they saw me. [*He opens the window and calls out:*] WHATTA YOU WANT?

MRS. DALLY [*Annoyed*]:   I told you to watch it, Frankie.

FRANKIE: WHAT? . . . They wanta know what I'm doing up here. [*She throws him a significant look.*] I'M . . . [*Thinking fast*] I'M FIXING THE LADY'S ICEBOX! [*This elicits another look of some significance.*] OKAY, HER REFRIGERATOR! . . . She says don't call it an icebox, call it a refrigerator. My old man always says icebox and my mother says it's not an icebox, it's a refrigerator; she's got the kids doin' it now. . . . WHAT? . . . YEAH, IT WAS BROKEN! . . . YEAH, IT'S ALL FIXED NOW! . . . NO, I CAN'T COME DOWN AND PLAY WITH YOU, I GOTTA GO TO WORK SOON. . . . WHAT? . . . WHAT DO YOU WANT A QUARTER FOR? . . . IT'LL PUT YA OFF YOUR SUPPER, CANDY. . . . YEAH? [*He takes a coin from his pocket.*] HERE! AND DON'T TELL MAMA! [*He tosses the coin into the yard.*] ANGIE, YOU SPLIT THAT WITH MARIA, YOU HEAR? . . . ANGIE? . . . [*But they are gone, apparently.*] Nutty kids. [*He closes the window.*]

MRS. DALLY: My refrigerator ain't the *only* thing around here that could use fixin'.

FRANKIE: You mean it's really busted?

MRS. DALLY: No, but I mean the whole place. What a dump.

FRANKIE: It's not so bad. I seen worse.

MRS. DALLY: *Tobacco Road*, maybe.

FRANKIE: What's that?

MRS. DALLY: Before your time. I mean, you never saw a place like this in no technicolor movie, right? You know, I once subscribed to *House Beautiful* for a solid year? It didn't do much good though. What the hell, it's like everything else: you either got it or you haven't, and if you got it you don't have to read about how to get it.

FRANKIE: Yeah, but what if you *haven't* got it?

MRS. DALLY: You can't afford it, anyway. . . . Here y'are. [*She proffers the shirt. He removes the sweater and puts the shirt on. She stands and begins fastening the buttons for him.*] Frankie . . . why did you want to know if I loved him?

FRANKIE: I just wondered.

MRS. DALLY: No particular reason. [*He shakes his head.*] Do you think I look as old as I said I am?

FRANKIE: No, I thought you was even younger.

MRS. DALLY: You know I still get the eye when I walk down the street in the right dress.

FRANKIE: You don't have to tell me, I watched you plenty of times.

MRS. DALLY: And the whistles—you never whistled.

FRANKIE: Well, you know, you livin' in the same building, I didn't think I better take a chance.

MRS. DALLY: That's one good thing about all the new buildings going up now.

FRANKIE: What?

MRS. DALLY: You know, those construction guys. They got no inhibitions. I mean, if a girl needs a lift all she hasta do is walk by one of those new buildings during lunch hour. I do that every once in a while. You can really depend on those guys to make you feel like you still got something to look at. That's a funny thing about these businessmen though, you

know? In my whole life I don't think I ever been whistled at
by a guy wearin' a suit and tie.

FRANKIE: It isn't gentlemanly.

MRS. DALLY: Yeah, well, I bet if they once in a while whistled
at a nice-looking fanny they wouldn't have so many heart at-
tacks.

[*The buttoning is completed.*]

FRANKIE: You think they'll hold this time?

MRS. DALLY: I wouldn't promise anything. [*She adds:*] But
you know what I don't like?

FRANKIE [*Lost*]:   What?

MRS. DALLY: What I don't like is the dirty remarks.

FRANKIE: Oh. Yeah.

MRS. DALLY: I remember once, this guy shouts, "Hey blondie!
how about it?"—I was blond then—so I turned around and I
said, "How about *what?*" You know, real nasty. You shoulda
seen the look on his face. He was embarrassed! Men! They're
all talk and not much action.

FRANKIE: Oh, yeah?

MRS. DALLY: Present company excepted. It's the truth,
though. Women got a lot more imagination than men. In
bed, I mean.

FRANKIE: You think so?

MRS. DALLY: No question.

FRANKIE: How many women you been in bed with?

MRS. DALLY [*With feigned offense*]:   Don't be smart. [*He
smiles; so does she.*] Anyway, you know what I mean.

FRANKIE: Maybe you better explain it to me.

MRS. DALLY: You've had enough "explaining" for one day.
What a waste. He's got no class, the brute. [*This, ruefully, at
the sweater she's just folded. She starts toward the bedroom.*]
You know what I'd like to do right now?

FRANKIE: What? [*She disappears into the bedroom without
answering and, in a moment, returns.*] What?

MRS. DALLY: I'd like to go for a walk. Down by the river,
maybe.

FRANKIE: Is that a hint I should get outa here?

MRS. DALLY: I mean with you, silly. Both of us.

FRANKIE: Oh.

MRS. DALLY: You realize, Frankie, all the time you been . . . coming here, all this time, and we never once been outside this place.

FRANKIE: Once. [*Pause. She seems evasive and does not respond.*] That time in the park. When the two old guys were singin' the Christmas carols. You forget?

MRS. DALLY: No, I didn't forget.

FRANKIE: You thought I forgot, huh? So whatta we have to go outside for, anyhow?

MRS. DALLY: Don't you ever go for walks with girls?

FRANKIE: Sure.

MRS. DALLY: So?

FRANKIE: Yeah, but that's different.

MRS. DALLY: How is it different?

FRANKIE: Well, you know . . . with you and me . . . it's different.

MRS. DALLY: Would you feel funny?

FRANKIE: How?

MRS. DALLY: You know, to go around places with me?

FRANKIE: What places?

MRS. DALLY: Just around. For walks. The movies. The museum, maybe.

FRANKIE: The museum!

MRS. DALLY: Would you, Frankie? Would you feel funny? With me?

FRANKIE: No, but I mean, suppose somebody saw us?

MRS. DALLY: It's a big city, Frankie.

FRANKIE: Well, it's just I never thought about it.

MRS. DALLY [*After a pause; defeated*]:   Oh, I guess it ain't worth taking the chance.

FRANKIE: You can't ever tell, somebody *might* see us.

MRS. DALLY: I didn't mean that.

FRANKIE: What?

MRS. DALLY [*Wryly*]:   I mean people thinking, look at the nice young man and his mother.

FRANKIE [*Gently*]:   Don't say that.

MRS. DALLY: Why? I bet you've thought it plenty of times.

FRANKIE [*Forcefully*]:   I never have.

MRS. DALLY [*Disbelieving*]   Oh, I know, I know.

FRANKIE: I'm telling you I never thought that! I just never thought about it, that's all . . . taking a walk. How should I know you wanta go for a walk, for chrissake? You usually got something else on your mind, far as I can see.

MRS. DALLY: Not always.

FRANKIE: Okay. Now I know. So you wanta go out? You just tell me where to meet you and I'll meet you there.

MRS. DALLY: No.

FRANKIE: Why not?

MRS. DALLY: I told you why.

FRANKIE: I don't care what anybody thinks.

MRS. DALLY: You don't have to, Frankie.

FRANKIE: I know I don't.

MRS. DALLY: I mean I *do*.

FRANKIE: Why?

MRS. DALLY: Let's forget it, now.

FRANKIE: You tell me where you want me to meet you. Someplace downtown?

MRS. DALLY: Stop! [*Her vehemence silences him; pause.*]

FRANKIE: Just remember who didn't want to go out. [*Pause.*]

MRS. DALLY: I should know better. A lotta times, you can't have the whole pie, you settle for a piece of it.

FRANKIE: Maybe I better go? [*She looks quickly at him.*] I mean he'll be getting home soon.

MRS. DALLY: You know he don't get home till after six.

FRANKIE [*Confessing the truth*]:   Well, I figured maybe you wanted me to take off.

MRS. DALLY: No. We been having a nice afternoon, Frankie.

FRANKIE: Yeah.

MRS. DALLY: Haven't we?

FRANKIE: Till you started worrying. I didn't know you were a worrier.

MRS. DALLY: There's a lotta things you didn't know.

FRANKIE: That's true.

MRS. DALLY: And what's the matter with the museum, by the way?

FRANKIE: What?

MRS. DALLY: The museum. I said maybe we could go to the museum, you looked like I said cemetery or something. You probably never even *been* to a museum.

FRANKIE: Sure I have. I was once to the Museum of Natural History. In the sixth grade. The whole class went.

MRS. DALLY: The sixth grade. That's what I thought.

FRANKIE: I didn't like it, anyway.

MRS. DALLY: Why not?

FRANKIE: Ah, I don't know . . . everything was . . . dead. [*She laughs.*] It *was*.

MRS. DALLY: Maybe *you'll* end up like that someday, sweetheart. Someone'll dig up your bones and hang 'em in a museum.

FRANKIE [*Excitedly, since she has put it in words for him*]:   I know! That's exactly what I meant. I wouldn't like it.

MRS. DALLY: That isn't the museum I meant, anyway. I'd show you something that's *alive*.

[*A knock on the door; both are startled, of course. A beat, and again the knock. He opens his mouth to speak but she gestures him to silence.*]

VOICE [*Off-stage*]:   Mrs. Dally! Are you there? [*Knocking again.*] Mrs. Dally! . . .

[*Silence for a moment, then a door is heard to slam across the hall.*]

MRS. DALLY: She wanted to invite me in for tea, probably. About once a week she traps me and I gotta drink her tea and listen to that phony English accent. Boy! is she a phony. She thinks when she sweats it's Chanel Number Five. That type.

When we first come here to live she used to call me Mrs.
Dawley. [*Mimicking broadly:*] "Oh, good afternoon, Mrs.
Dawley." Finally I said, *"Dally."* She said, "I *beg* your pardon." I said, *"Dally.* Like in dally awhile?" She looked kinda
disappointed.

FRANKIE: What were you gonna show me? [*She stares vaguely
at him.*] Something alive, you said.

MRS. DALLY: Oh, yeah. . . . It's a beautiful thing, Frankie.
It's a cup.

FRANKIE: A cup?

MRS. DALLY: Yeah, a kind of a cup. A man made it a long
time ago. His name was Cellini, he was Italian.

FRANKIE: Oh, then it must be good.

MRS. DALLY: No, listen, now. Listen. . . . This cup . . . it's
all gold. Solid gold. And it's covered with all kinds of jewels,
every kind, diamonds and rubies and emeralds, I don't know
what all. But that isn't what's so great about it. It's the pearl.
A part of the cup, the way it's made, kinda hangs over *into*
the cup, you see, and then, hanging from that is this pearl.
One little pearl. And you know what? The way he made it,
this pearl never stop moving. I mean, the cup is in a glass
case and you can't touch it and it's been there for I don't
know how long, absolutely still, but the pearl *moves*. It . . .
trembles. I mean, it's balanced so perfect that it feels, you
know, vibrations, that're so soft *we* don't even feel them. In
the earth. But this pearl feels them and it *moves*. I mean,
maybe somebody closes a door on the other side of the world
. . . and the pearl feels it.

FRANKIE: That's pretty smart.

MRS. DALLY: No, don't you see, Frankie. That this man
could make something like that move forever. After he's dead,
and forever. Like it was *alive*.

FRANKIE: I'll go and see that.

MRS. DALLY [*Dreamily*]:   If a butterfly has a heart I think it
beats like that. . . . [*Then, returning to him:*] Will you.
Frankie? Go see it?

FRANKIE: If you come.

MRS. DALLY: But even if I don't, will you?

FRANKIE: Okay.

MRS. DALLY: It'll make me very happy.

FRANKIE: Why?

MRS. DALLY: Because it's important to see something like that, Frankie. It's important to know about it. When you see it . . . you'll see what I mean.

FRANKIE: I'm gonna feel kinda funny standing there staring at a . . . a nervous pearl.

MRS. DALLY [*Disappointedly*]:   Oh, Frankie. . . .

FRANKIE: I'm only foolin'. I know what you mean.

MRS. DALLY: You'll see.

FRANKIE: I didn't think you was the museum type.

MRS. DALLY: No.

FRANKIE: How come?

MRS. DALLY: Oh . . . it's cool and quiet. And it's full of beautiful things. And people who like beautiful things. I don't go hardly ever, any more.

FRANKIE: Why?

MRS. DALLY: Hafta come back here sooner or later. Only, after that, it looks even worse. That's the trouble with beautiful things when you don't have them.

FRANKIE: You can always look.

MRS. DALLY [*Pleased; eagerly*]:   That's right, Frankie! That's right. You can always look. And don't ever forget it.

FRANKIE [*Abruptly*]:   You happy right now?

MRS. DALLY [*Taken back momentarily*]:   Why?

FRANKIE: Sometimes you look happy about the damnedest things.

MRS. DALLY: It's one of my two virtues.

FRANKIE: What's the other one?

MRS. DALLY: I don't know, but I know I must have at least two.

FRANKIE: No, I mean it though.

MRS. DALLY: *What* do you mean?

FRANKIE: The things that make you happy.

MRS. DALLY: How do you know what makes me happy? [*She adds quickly:*] Well, you know one thing that makes me happy.

FRANKIE: Yeah, but what else, I mean.

MRS. DALLY: I already told you some things.

FRANKIE [*Impatiently*]:   The pearl . . .

MRS. DALLY: And the George Washington Bridge, don't forget the George Washington Bridge.

FRANKIE: But I don't mean them. I mean like when I say something.

MRS. DALLY [*Slyly*]:   Oh, well, that's just that you ain't much of a talker, sweetheart, so when you say something, anything at all, I get all giggly about it.

FRANKIE: Come on!

MRS. DALLY: What?

FRANKIE: All I said was there's no law against looking and a stupid thing like that makes you happy.

MRS. DALLY: Some people ain't as smart as they think they are, Frankie. You, you ain't as dumb as you think you are.

FRANKIE: I don't think I'm dumb. Whatta you mean?

MRS. DALLY: I'll explain it to you someday, maybe.

FRANKIE: Why don't you explain it right now?

MRS. DALLY: I wonder how many somedays we got left.

FRANKIE: What?

MRS. DALLY: What makes *you* happy, Frankie?

FRANKIE: Me?

MRS. DALLY: Yeah, you.

FRANKIE: I don't know.

MRS. DALLY: Whatta you mean, you don't know. You never felt happy in your life?

FRANKIE: Sure, I felt happy.

MRS. DALLY: Well, what was it made you feel that way?

FRANKIE: I don't remember.

MRS. DALLY: It was that long ago?

FRANKIE: No, it wasn't long ago.

MRS. DALLY: When?

FRANKIE: I don't know! I mean, what's the difference?

MRS. DALLY: There's a *lotta* difference, Frankie. What's the good of feeling happy if you don't remember it!

FRANKIE: I re*member*, for chrissake!

MRS. DALLY: Why don't you tell me, then?

FRANKIE: Because it sounds stupid! I mean, you're making me feel embarrassed!

[*Pause.*]

MRS. DALLY [*Retreating*]: Oh. . . . Well, I didn't mean to make you feel embarrassed. I'm sorry. [*She takes the album from the table and disappears quickly with it into the bedroom;* FRANKIE *is thoughtful. She reenters.*] You want me to fix you a sandwich before you go to work?

FRANKIE: When the kids were going for their candy.

MRS. DALLY: What?

FRANKIE: I felt happy when the kids were going for their candy.

MRS. DALLY: Let's forget it. *I'm* beginnin' to feel stupid. [*They are back to back now, he at the table, she with her hand on the refrigerator door.*]

FRANKIE: You asked me, I'm tellin' ya.

MRS. DALLY: Okay. You want a sandwich?

FRANKIE: I don't mean when I gave them the quarter, either.

MRS. DALLY: You want a sandwich before you go?

FRANKIE: I mean after that, when they took off down the alley.

MRS. DALLY [*Flatly*]: Yeah.

FRANKIE: Watchin' them run to *get* the candy, that's what made me feel happy.

[*Pause.*]

MRS. DALLY: Do you want—

FRANKIE: No, just a beer, if you got any. [*She gets the beer from the refrigerator, and a glass; goes to the table and pours.*] And the last thing before that that made me feel happy was listening to you before.

MRS. DALLY: When?

FRANKIE: The noise you were making. In there. With me.

MRS. DALLY: Now *I'm* embarrassed.

FRANKIE: You asked me.

[*A pause before she is able to speak.*]

MRS. DALLY: I'm glad that's one of the things makes you happy. [*She touches him briefly and sits.*] Frankie . . . did you ever wonder if I did this before?

FRANKIE: Did what?

MRS. DALLY: This. You and me. Did you ever wonder? [*He shrugs and shakes his head, but not very definitely.*] I didn't. I been married fifteen years. I'm just telling you in case you think I make a habit.

FRANKIE: How come now?

MRS. DALLY: Oh . . . I guess some people are time bombs, Frankie.

FRANKIE: You sorry or something? You look sorry all of a sudden.

MRS. DALLY: It's a sin, Frankie. I think about that sometimes.

FRANKIE [*Incredulous*]:   You believe in that stuff?

MRS. DALLY: I was raised a good Catholic, Frankie.

FRANKIE: So all you hafta do is go to confession.

MRS. DALLY: Sweetheart, I *been* confessing you. Every week. And Father Shields is getting pretty annoyed.

FRANKIE [*Slyly*]:   We could always stop.

MRS. DALLY [*Quickly*]:   I didn't say anything about that, did I? [*He smiles slowly.*] Fresh kid! [*She smiles in spite of herself.*] Besides, it's a sin for you too.

FRANKIE: *I* ain't married.

MRS. DALLY: Yeah, well . . . you're corrupting my morals, or something.

FRANKIE: I'm pretty special then, huh?

MRS. DALLY: Why?

FRANKIE: If you never did it before.

[*Pause.*]

MRS. DALLY: Yes, you're special, Frankie.

FRANKIE: Why me?

MRS. DALLY: Why are you special?

FRANKIE: No, I mean, why me, why not somebody else?

MRS. DALLY: Nobody knows the answer to that one, Frankie. [*She adds, mocking herself:*] Not even me, smart as I am. [*She rises abruptly.*] I don't know, you ain't even good-looking.

FRANKIE: What's the matter?

MRS. DALLY [*Gathering the cups and saucers*]:   Nothing's the matter. [*She goes quickly to the sink with them.*]

FRANKIE: Listen, I'm not so bad-lookin', am I?

MRS. DALLY: I've seen worse.

FRANKIE: Thanks a lot.

MRS. DALLY: I'm only teasing, baby.

FRANKIE: I was just about to take back what I said about *your* looks.

MRS. DALLY: Once you say it, you can't take it back.

FRANKIE: I could if I didn't mean it in the first place. [*Pause.*]

MRS. DALLY: Didn't you?

FRANKIE: That'll teach you to knock my looks.

MRS. DALLY: Frankie, didn't you mean it?

FRANKIE: Oh, now whatta you think! Sure I meant it. *I* can't tease *you?*

MRS. DALLY: Fresh kid. [*She turns again to the sink; he approaches her from behind, putting his arms about her.*]

FRANKIE: Aren't you glad I'm such a *nice* fresh kid, though.

MRS. DALLY [*Ironically*]:   I'm just lucky, I guess. My momma tells me I was born that way. [*She turns to face him.*] Frankie . . . you won't ever tell me anything you don't mean, will you?

FRANKIE: No.

MRS. DALLY: You never have, have you?

FRANKIE: No. Why should I?

MRS. DALLY: It's a very important thing, Frankie.

FRANKIE: I'm no liar.

MRS. DALLY: I don't mean that, it's not the same thing as lying. It's something different. It's like if I say to somebody, "How are you?" when I don't really care how they are. Or if I say, "It was nice meeting you"—if it wasn't. Just because you're supposed to say things like that. You see what I mean? You don't ever have to tell me something you don't mean.

FRANKIE: Okay.

MRS. DALLY: It's an important thing.

FRANKIE: Okay, but I don't see any harm in just being polite.

MRS. DALLY: No, no, there's no harm in just being polite. But I mean with you and me. If you start saying things to *me* just to be polite . . . that's no good.

FRANKIE: What about you?

MRS. DALLY: You don't have to worry about me.

FRANKIE: Why?

MRS. DALLY: You're the one goes out that door these afternoons. I stay here.

FRANKIE: So?

MRS. DALLY: So if some afternoon I'm waiting for you to come in the door and you don't . . . being polite to you won't change it. [*Pause.*] You still don't understand?

FRANKIE: I guess I'm not so smart as you thought I was, after all.

MRS. DALLY: Well . . . you'll understand soon enough.

FRANKIE: Anyway, I don't see why you need me to tell you you're good-looking.

MRS. DALLY: Don't you, now.

FRANKIE: You got him around *all* the time for that.

MRS. DALLY: The last time he told me I was beautiful was around nineteen forty-eight.

FRANKIE: Don't exaggerate.

MRS. DALLY: I don't have to.

[*Pause. He scrutinizes her.*]

FRANKIE: Hey, listen, were you really in show business?

MRS. DALLY: What?

FRANKIE: You told me you were in show business once.

MRS. DALLY: Yeah.

FRANKIE: You really did a—an act?

MRS. DALLY: You don't believe me?

FRANKIE: Sure, I believe you.

MRS. DALLY: I once did twenty-seven weeks at the Club 16 on Ocean Parkway. Broke a record. The Ha Ha Club, Flatbush Avenue, I almost broke a record there, sixteen weeks. How come you don't believe me?

FRANKIE: I *believe* you.

[*She looks cautiously at him for a moment before she continues.*]

MRS. DALLY: Anyway, he made me give it up after we got married. He said it was silly-looking for a girl to be playing a trombone.

FRANKIE: A trombone!

MRS. DALLY: Yeah.

FRANKIE: You played a *trombone?*

MRS. DALLY [*Wearily, at this familiar reaction*]: Yeah, I played a trombone.

FRANKIE: No, it's okay, I just didn't know you played the trombone.

MRS. DALLY: I sang and danced, too. I mean, it was all part of the act. I should never've given it up. . . . But then I had the kid, you know, and after I lost him it was too late to start all over again. Not that I ever would've been great, you know, I mean really big or anything, but . . .

FRANKIE: What?

MRS. DALLY: Well . . . it would've been something to do. Listen, you sure you believe me?

FRANKIE: Certainly, I believe you! Whatta you want me to do? [*Then, offhandedly:*] It's just you said you were gonna show me it.

MRS. DALLY: Show you what?

FRANKIE: Your act.

MRS. DALLY: Sweetheart, I didn't say I'd show you my act, I said I'd do a number for you sometime.

FRANKIE: Okay, a number.

MRS. DALLY: I will.

FRANKIE: When?

MRS. DALLY: I have to practice some more.

FRANKIE: You been practicing?

MRS. DALLY: Certainly.

FRANKIE: Why?

MRS. DALLY: I haven't done it all these years, you expect me to do it without practicing a little?

FRANKIE: But I mean I didn't think you were gonna go to all that trouble.

MRS. DALLY: You didn't.

FRANKIE: No. . . . So do it.

MRS. DALLY: I will.

FRANKIE: No, I mean now.

MRS. DALLY: Now!

FRANKIE: Yeah, why not? [*She shakes her head.*] C'mon! You must've practiced enough.

MRS. DALLY: No.

FRANKIE: Oh, come on, don't be modest.

MRS. DALLY: I'm not modest. [*She adds:*] I mean, I *am* modest. But that's not the reason. It's not good enough yet, that's all.

FRANKIE: It's good enough for me.

MRS. DALLY: No.

FRANKIE: Okay. I won't beg for it.

MRS. DALLY: You really want to hear it? [*He looks at her, exasperated.*] All right. [*She rises and starts toward the bedroom.*]

FRANKIE: Where you going?

MRS. DALLY: Remember, it probably won't be as good as if I had a little more practice. [*Disappears into the bedroom.*]

FRANKIE: You want me to do anything?

MRS. DALLY [*Off*]: All you have to do is not expect too much.

FRANKIE: No, I mean do you want me to pull down the window shades, or anything?

[*Her head appears from behind the drape.*]

MRS. DALLY: What kind of an act do you think it is? [*She disappears again, and in a moment the trombone is heard, a random, tentative warming-up; then, in the spirit of the thing, a fanfare, and she appears, sweeping aside the drape, trombone held aloft.* FRANKIE *applauds.*] I should be dressed.

FRANKIE: That's okay.

MRS. DALLY: Picture gold lamé. [*He nods.*] Red satin shoes.

FRANKIE: Nice.

MRS. DALLY: I come down in front of the band . . . [*She places the band for him with a gesture.*] . . . this is after I'm introduced, naturally. Then a few gags, a few jokes about the band, how lousy they are, that's always good for a laugh. Then you say you'd like to open the show with an old favorite—you always figure any song that was written before yesterday is an old favorite—the music comes up behind me. . . . [*She hums the orchestra's introduction to the tune, then begins to sing. The song is "After You've Gone," in a moderately slow tempo. After one chorus, she lifts the trombone to her lips and goes into the next chorus, very fast, very razzmatazz.* FRANKIE *becomes caught up and begins to drum on the table; fortunately, he has a nice sense of rhythm and the effect isn't at all bad. Her ending is loud and, musically, very involved.* FRANKIE's *applause is enthusiastic and she receives it awkwardly, her acceptance half serious, half comic.*] That gives you an idea.

FRANKIE [*Jokingly*]:   You could make a comeback!

[*They become aware now of a knocking from above that has been heard throughout the last few bars of the number, and since. They gaze at the ceiling; the noise stops abruptly.*]

MRS. DALLY: Mrs. Schmidt would sooner I didn't. [*Feeling suddenly awkward and self-conscious, she starts quickly for the bedroom.*]

FRANKIE: That was really damned good.

MRS. DALLY: I should've been dressed right.

FRANKIE: No, I got the picture very good.

MRS. DALLY: If this was the movies I would've had a thousand-piece invisible orchestra. [*She enters the bedroom.*]

FRANKIE: Listen, I mean it, you were really good. [*He rises with his empty beer bottle, takes it to the sink, then goes to the refrigerator and gets another bottle. His glance falls on a book lying on top of the refrigerator; he takes it up and is gazing at the title when* MRS. DALLY *emerges from the bedroom.*] What's this? *The Love Poems of John Donne.* [*He pronounces the name as written.*]

MRS. DALLY [*Startled*]:   That wouldn't interest you. Give it to me.

FRANKIE: Why? What is it?

MRS. DALLY: A book of poems. Obviously. [*Her hand is extended for the book.*]

FRANKIE: Who's John Donne?

MRS. DALLY [*Correcting him*]:   Donne. He's a poet.

BOTH [*In unison*]:   Obviously.

MRS. DALLY: Give it to me, Frankie.

FRANKIE: Why? What's the big secret? They dirty or something?

MRS. DALLY: No, they aren't dirty or something. They just wouldn't interest you, that's all. I forgot and left it there by accident.

FRANKIE: Is it yours?

MRS. DALLY: Yes, it's mine. Frankie, will you give me the book.
[*They are moving slowly about the room now and* FRANKIE *has the book opened.*]

FRANKIE [*Reading, badly*]:   "Mark but this flea, and mark in this/How little that which thou deny'st me is;/It sucked me first, and now sucks thee,/ . . ."

MRS. DALLY: Give it to me, now, Frankie!

FRANKIE: ". . . And in this flea our two bloods mingled be;/ Thou know'st that this cannot be said/A sin, nor shame, nor loss of maidenhead . . ." Not dirty, huh?

MRS. DALLY: If you don't stop this minute—

FRANKIE [*He has turned to another page*]: "I wonder, by my troth, what thou and I/Did till we loved? Were we not weaned till then,/But sucked on country pleasures, childishly?/Or snorted we in the Seven Sleepers' den?/'Twas so; but this . . ." [*He trails off, noting her silent rage.*] What're you so excited about?

MRS. DALLY: You don't even know how to read it.

FRANKIE: What do you think I was just doing?

MRS. DALLY: Making fun of it. Like *him*.

[*Pause.*]

FRANKIE [*Quietly*]: I wasn't makin' fun of it. . . . Listen, what're you crying for?

MRS. DALLY: I'm not crying!

FRANKIE: I wasn't making fun of it. . . . I just don't know how to read it, then.

MRS. DALLY: You probably never even *saw* a poem before.

FRANKIE [*Simply*]: Yes, I did. We hadda read poetry in high school. *Paradise Lost* by Milton. I even hadda memorize some of it. You wanna hear it?

MRS. DALLY: Thanks anyway.

FRANKIE: Okay, so I don't know how to read a poem right.

MRS. DALLY: Boy! You sure don't.

FRANKIE [*Mildly challenging*]: You do though, huh?

MRS. DALLY [*Defiant*]: Yes.

FRANKIE: How do you know?

MRS. DALLY: I don't know how I know.

FRANKIE: Somebody tell you?

MRS. DALLY: Some people just *know* some things, that's all.

FRANKIE: Okay. [*He proffers the book, opened; she does not move.*] Go ahead, you do it.

MRS. DALLY: What?

FRANKIE: Read it.

MRS. DALLY: You don't believe me?

FRANKIE: You always think I don't believe you. Yeah, I believe you. But I wanta see what's the difference.

[*She hesitates still, then finally takes the book, apprehensive and suspicious of his motive. Finally, she begins to read; and she can.*]

MRS. DALLY:

"*I wonder, by my troth, what thou and I*
Did till we loved? Were we not weaned till then,
But sucked on country pleasures, childishly?
Or snorted we in the Seven Sleepers' den?
'Twas so; but this, all pleasures fancies be.

[*She lifts her eyes from the page and continues from memory.*]

"*If ever any beauty I did see,*
Which I desired, and got, 'twas but a dream of thee.

"*And now good morrow to our waking souls,*
Which watch not one another out of fear;
For love all love of other sights controls,
And makes one little room an everywhere.
Let sea discoverers to new worlds have gone;
Let maps to other, worlds on worlds have shown;
Let us possess one world; each hath one, and is one.

"*My face in thine eye, thine in mine appears,*
And true plain hearts do in the faces rest;
Where can we find two better hemispheres
Without sharp north, without declining west?
Whatever dies was not mixed equally;
If our two loves be one, or thou and I
Love so alike that none do slacken, none can die."

[*Pause; they are still,* FRANKIE *watching her steadily. She moves to the window and stands, looking out, her back to him.*] Beautiful dreamer, that's me.

FRANKIE: Why?

MRS. DALLY [*After a pause*]:   I told you a lie once, Frankie.

FRANKIE [*Referring back, lightly*]:   You mean you told me something you didn't mean?

MRS. DALLY: Oh, no. I never did that. . . . But I'm older than I said I was even. I'm thirty-eight years old.

FRANKIE [*After a pause*]:   Okay.

MRS. DALLY: And I love you, Frankie. [*She waits for him to speak.*] Stupid, huh? [*He still cannot answer.*] Isn't it?

FRANKIE [*Finally*]:   Considering me, yeah. I mean, I don't know why anyone would wanta love *me*.

MRS. DALLY: You're a kind young man, Frankie.

FRANKIE: Why? I mean it.

MRS. DALLY: I know you do. That's why you're kind. If you said that and didn't mean it, you'd be polite, but not kind. . . . I shouldn't've told you, I know that. . . .

FRANKIE: Why?

MRS. DALLY: But once you feel it, you can only go so long before you have to say it. It's like waiting for the other shoe to drop.

FRANKIE: Why shouldn't you've told me?

MRS. DALLY: Because once you say it, it can change everything.

FRANKIE: It don't change anything.

MRS. DALLY: It isn't enough just to be loved, sweetheart. You have to know what to do with it.

FRANKIE: So what do I have to *do* with it?

MRS. DALLY: That's what I mean.

FRANKIE [*Impatiently*]:   What? [*She only smiles, ruefully.*] Well, don't look at me like I'm an idiot! What!

MRS. DALLY: No, no, no! I wasn't doing that. I wasn't. The thing is . . . I can't tell you what to do with it. Nobody can. [*Now he understands; pause.*] I've been good to you, haven't I, Frankie?

FRANKIE: Sure you have.

MRS. DALLY: I've given you a lot of things.

FRANKIE: Yes. You'll get it all back, too.

MRS. DALLY: From you? [*He nods.*] No. . . . But maybe
someone else will . . . and that'll be just as good. [*Pause.*]
It's like that game we used to play when I was a kid: Pass It
On. You ever play that? You'd say something to the kid next
to you, or do something and tell him to pass it on. Sometimes
it was something nice, sometimes it was a punch in the arm.
Being alive is a lot like that game.

FRANKIE: I played that when I was a kid.

MRS. DALLY: Don't stop.

FRANKIE: Unless it's a punch in the arm.

MRS. DALLY: No, you'll pass those on too. . . . You remember you asked me why I picked you and not somebody else?

FRANKIE: You said you couldn't say.

MRS. DALLY: No. But I know why I wanted you to come back
after that first time . . . and all the times. You ever noticed
that very often people got ways of talking to each other to
avoid talking to each other?

FRANKIE: No . . . I don't think so.

MRS. DALLY: You listen, you'll see. But it was hardly ever
like that with you and me. Every once in a while in this life,
Frankie, somebody talks to somebody else. I mean, *talks.* It's
sweet music, Frankie. And you listen for it, you hear? Always,
your whole life, listen for it. [*Pause; he understands. She kisses
him seriously.*] You'd better get outa here, it's almost time.

FRANKIE: That isn't what I want to do.

MRS. DALLY: What do you want to do? [*He smiles.*] Tomorrow's another day.

FRANKIE: It's nice they arranged it like that.

MRS. DALLY: Beat it, fresh kid. [*She goes to the door, unlocks
it and looks into the hall; she closes the door, turns to him,
holding his coat, waiting. He approaches and takes the coat
from her.*]

FRANKIE: I'll see you tomorrow?

MRS. DALLY: I'll be here.
[*Pause.*]

FRANKIE: Do you *really* love *me?*

MRS. DALLY: No, I don't really love you, you're not even good-looking. Why aren't you wearing a scarf or something, you'll catch cold going around like that. [*She embraces him fiercely and kisses him; pause.*] One of these days you'll say that and I won't.

FRANKIE: What?

MRS. DALLY: One of these days you'll say, "I'll see you tomorrow," and I won't.

FRANKIE: Stop, will ya.

MRS. DALLY: Just remember what I said: listen to the sweet music . . . and pass it on. [*She opens the door; he looks quickly into the hall, then at her, and goes out. She closes the door slowly. She goes to the table, takes up the book and the hairbrush and starts toward the bedroom, slowly brushing her hair.*]

CURTAIN

The Rook
Lawrence Osgood

CAST:

Edna .... Estelle Omens
Alf .... Robert Dryden
Rico .... Paul Savior
Adele .... Jessica Walter

Directed by Joseph Hardy

First presented at Theater 1964 Playwrights Unit Workshop,
January 19, 1964.

THE TIME: *The present, late on a fall night.*
SCENE: *A corner of Washington Square Park, New York.*

People in the Play:

ALF
EDNA
RICO
ADELE

An overhead lamp shines on two men sitting on benches
at one side of the stage with a concrete checkerboard table
between them. They are playing chess. A single bench faces
the audience on the other side of the stage. Upstage, be-
tween them, may be one or two other arrangements of con-
crete table and benches.
Of the two men, one has his back partially turned to the

*audience. He is clearly a young man. His coat fits him well,
he wears no hat, but he does wear gloves. He plays the game
casually but with great skill, never hesitating over a move
and moving the pieces swiftly and precisely. This is* RICO.
*The other man is in his fifties. He is bundled up in a baggy
overcoat and wears a winter hat. He also wears mitten-
gloves. Except for wild spurts, he plays slowly, always trying to see through the other's moves before making his own.
Because he usually fails in this, he moves his own pieces
nervously or lingeringly, but sometimes, when he thinks he
has succeeded, with a flourish of triumph. He loves the game
with a deep, frustrated passion. This is* ALF. *His wife* EDNA
is sitting on the single bench, wrapped in a blanket.

A game is well advanced, and it is ALF's *move. He makes
it nervously.* RICO *glances at the board, makes a quick move,
lights a cigarette.*

ALF [*Looking at* RICO *and then at the board*]:   Don't know
what you did that for. [*He hesitates, then makes a move.*]
RICO [*Moving*]:   Checkmate.
[ALF *stares in disbelief at the board, then slumps. Failure fills
his mind.* RICO *picks up his cigarettes,* EDNA *gathers her blanket
about her.* ALF *rallies.*]
ALF: Time for another?
EDNA: Alfie, not another!
RICO: Anything you say, Alf.
EDNA: But it's two o'clock in the morning.
RICO [*Lightly*]:   Not even midnight, Edna.
ALF: You go along. We'll only play this game.
EDNA: If I stay here, that's all you'll play. Otherwise you'll
be up all night. Oh no, if you want to be Scott of the Ant-
arctic, Alfie, I'll be your Ice Maiden.
ALF: Suit yourself.
EDNA: As if that ever happened. . . . Off in his own little
world of kings and queens and knights and bishops. Oh, and
castles. I almost forgot the castles.

ALF: Rooks. You should call them "rooks."

EDNA: "Rooks" is the word.

RICO: You're first, Alf.

[*Throughout their own and* EDNA's *dialogue that follows,* RICO *and* ALF *continue playing.*]

EDNA: Let a man have his hobby, they say. Takes his mind off his work, they say. Relaxes him. That's what they say. They should see my Alfie go through his dinner. *I* haven't seen him do it for years. As soon as I sit down, he's up. . . . Correspondence matches. Fourteen people he plays chess with through the mails. Names on postcards is all they are. And for them, he leaves me sitting at the dinner table. Every night, a six-o'clock widow. . . . I'd like to have a word with those newspaper people. Those "Make Your Husband Happy with a Hobby" people. . . . And is he even winning any of those fourteen correspondence matches through the mails? . . . Normal people play chess indoors. Normal people don't have fourteen correspondence matches spread all over their living room so they have to go outdoors for an ordinary game, spring, summer, winter, and fall. . . . I don't mind it so much in the summer. It's warm in the summer. At least there are other people in the park at two o'clock in the morning in the summer.

RICO: Midnight, Edna.

EDNA: Of course, what they're doing in the park at two o'clock in the morning in the summer is something else. None of my business, really. But I must say, the things I've seen, with people sitting, or lying, on all those benches at two A.M. in the summer, when it's hot. . . . They're not playing chess, not them. . . . Oh well . . . [*Pulls blanket tighter.*] Where *is* Adele?

RICO [*Lightly*]:   She'll be here.

EDNA: But will she bring the coffee?

RICO: That's what she went for.

EDNA: I am aware that's what she went for. What I'd like to know is, will she bring it back?

RICO: She'll bring it back.

EDNA: Send her to the store for oleomargarine when she was a little girl, likely as not she'd bring back soap. Not even from the same store.

RICO: Edna, she's not a little girl any more. She's my girl now, remember?

EDNA: I suppose you've been giving her a memory course?

RICO: She went for the coffee, Edna; she'll bring back the coffee.

[*Pause; the men play.*]

EDNA: Couldn't get butter in those days. That was during the war. Alfie enlisted. Overage, of course. But they took him. They took him.

ALF: Edna, I'm trying to think.

EDNA: Well, it's a wonder your brain cells aren't congealed. Dragging us all out here in the subzero weather.

RICO [*Lightly*]:   Upper forties, Edna.

EDNA: Who says it's the upper forties?

RICO: Weather man. Low tonight in the upper forties. I checked.

EDNA: Is the weather man sitting outdoors at two A.M. in the morning? Sound asleep in a nice warm bed, that's where the weather man is. Don't tell me he knows what's going on. [*Pause.*] So you checked the weather, did you?

ALF: Edna, will you kindly go away? We're trying to play chess.

EDNA: And where do you suggest I go?

ALF: If you won't go home, sit on the bench.

EDNA: I've been sitting on that bench, Alfie, till my blanket's worn out.

ALF: Walk, then.

EDNA: I *am* walking.

ALF: Well, walk someplace else.

EDNA: Maybe I will. Down to the docks, that's where I'll walk to. Where the ships come in. It's a good night for that. Full moon, partly cloudy skies. Or maybe to one of those warehouses where they back up the trucks to the platforms and unload things in the dark. It's a good night for that too, isn't it, Rico?

RICO: If you say so, Edna.

EDNA: You mean, if the weather man says so.

ALF: For Chrissake, what's all this about the weather man? Edna, for the last time, will you leave us alone?

EDNA: You! You wouldn't care if it was Molotov cocktails or poisoned olive oil, would you? I wouldn't be surprised if they were unloading something like that right now. In one of those darkened warehouses over by the river. But I don't suppose it's ever even entered your head to ask that son-in-law of yours what kind of things his company sells to people. Kings and queens and knights and bishops. Ask him, ask him what they sell to the unsuspecting public, and see if you get a straight answer. That'll be a frosty Friday. Oh, something funny's going on all the time with those consignments of his, believe you me. Adele says the same thing.

RICO: Is that right? You must have supersonic hearing, Edna. Like dogs have.

EDNA: A mother knows when her little girl's upset.

RICO: And a husband knows when his mother-in-law is being a—[*Stops himself.*] Go on, Alf. Move.

ALF: It's your move.

RICO: Oh. OK. [*As he studies his move.*] Item: The company I work for does not do business on partly cloudy nights in darkened warehouses. Nor is the company I work for run by the weather man. [*Pause.*] Item number two: My wife Adele, who left us a few moments ago to get us coffee, is not only happy in her marriage, but also possesses a normal brain and will presently return to us, bringing the coffee.

[*During the pause in* RICO's *speech,* EDNA *has begun to hum* "Carolina Moon." *By the end of it, she is singing.*]

ALF: Edna!

[EDNA *goes back to humming. The men play,* EDNA *hums.*

ADELE *enters. She is a pretty girl, blonde, eager to please. She comes in out of breath.*]

ADELE: I got the coffee.

EDNA: Well, let's have it. [*Takes coffee from* ADELE, *who goes to* RICO.]

ADELE: Hi.

RICO: Hi.

EDNA: Black. Regular. Light. What's this one?

ADELE: What?

EDNA: What's this fourth coffee? I can't read the writing.

ADELE: What are the other three?

EDNA: Black, regular, and light.

ADELE: Golly, I don't remember. Taste it. Rico takes his black.

EDNA [*Tasting*]:   Heavy on the sugar. That'll be Alfie's.

ADELE: Honey, can I tell you something that happened while I was getting the coffee?

EDNA: Since when do you take your coffee light?

ADELE: It was very weird.

RICO: Go ahead.

EDNA: Adele, I'm talking to you.

ADELE: I'm sorry. What did you say?

EDNA: I said, since when do you take your coffee light?

ADELE: I don't. [*Turning back to* RICO.] Well, I was—

EDNA: Well, I don't either.

ADELE: I was on my way to the coffee shop, and—

EDNA: Adele, will you come over here, please. There's something I want to ask you.

RICO: Go on. You can bring me back my coffee.

[ADELE *goes to* EDNA.]

EDNA: There's one regular left and one light. Whose is the light?

ADELE: Isn't that Daddy's?

EDNA: His is the heavy on the sugar.

ADELE: Oh.

EDNA: I didn't ask for my coffee light, Adele.

ADELE: Daddy, how do you want your coffee?

ALF: Regular's OK.

ADELE: Oh. I thought you wanted it light.

EDNA: He'll take the heavy on the sugar, you take the regular, and I'll take the light.

ADELE: But Daddy just said *he* wanted the regular.

EDNA: All right, he'll take the regular, I'll take—Adele, I do wish you'd remember things a little better. It makes it very difficult for other people, you know.

ADELE: Well, I'm sorry. But something happened to me on the way there, and I guess I got a little mixed up.

EDNA: Something was always happening to you on the way to get things, Adele, that got you mixed up. I was just telling Rico that.

ADELE: Mommy, what did you tell him a thing like that for?

EDNA: Hasn't he a right to know what you were like when you were a little girl?

ADELE: I suppose so.

EDNA: Now, where were we?

ADELE: Daddy was taking the regular.

EDNA: All right. He'll take the regular, I'll take the heavy on the sugar, and you take the light.

ADELE: Are you sure you wouldn't rather have the light?

EDNA [*Exasperated*]: Do you want your coffee heavy on the sugar, regular, or light, Alfie? Those are the choices.

ALF: What are?

EDNA: Heavy on the sugar, regular, or light.

ALF: Heavy on the sugar.

EDNA: Really, Adele! Now I'll take your father his coffee, and you take Rico his. And when we've done that, you take the regular, and your poor old mother will take the light.
[*They divide up and deliver the coffees. The women sit on the benches next to their husbands.*]

RICO [*To* ADELE]: Tell me your story, honey. Tell me the

story of What Happened to Our Adele on Her Way To Get the Coffee.

ADELE: You really want to hear?

RICO: Sure I do.

ADELE: Well, I was walking down the street, and I was thinking about our new vacuum cleaner. It just popped into my head, and I was thinking how much I liked it and everything, when all of a sudden I notice this man coming toward me carrying a box. Well, right away I was curious, because the box looked exactly like the one our new vacuum cleaner came in. Well, he kept coming toward me and I kept going toward him, and when we passed, I took a good hard look at that box—but not so he'd notice, of course. And can you imagine how I felt when I saw it had "Wonderwhirl Vacuum Cleaner" written on it? I was fascinated. So I stopped and pretended to put a dime in a parking meter.

RICO: You what?

ADELE: Pretended to put a dime in a parking meter. What else could I do? Anyway, the next thing I knew, he stopped in front of a brownstone house, looked very carefully up and down the street—and I stood there with my dime, you know, perfectly natural, but watching him out of the corner of my eye—and then he gently put the box down on the steps going up to the front door and disappeared into the areaway underneath them. And pretty soon I heard noises coming from that areaway, like banging around. I didn't know what to think. But the next minute, up he comes again, with a garbage can! Well, as soon as I saw that garbage can, I knew he was going to look up and down the street again. I just knew that. So lickety-split I ducked behind a car that was parked there.

RICO: Dell, baby.

ADELE: Well, I didn't want him to see me. And I was right. Because when I peeked around that car, there he was, putting the box in the garbage can! [*Silence.*] Don't you think that was weird?

RICO: Yeah, that was, kind of.

ADELE: I thought so too. So I ducked back and waited a minute, and when I looked out again, he was gone. So then, I crept up to that garbage can—

RICO: And took off the lid and looked at the box. Dell, honey.

ADELE: But it was *our box!*

RICO: Our box. Come on, Dell, we're the only people in New York who ever bought a Wonderwhirl vacuum cleaner?

ADELE: Well, it certainly looked like our box. And anyway, I hadn't half recovered from that shock when the really weirdest thing happened.

ALF: Check.

ADELE: I was just going to open the box—

RICO [*To* ALF]: What?

ALF: I said "check."

ADELE: I was just going to open the box, Rico—

EDNA: Don't interrupt your father's game, Adele.

RICO [*After making a quick move*]: Go on.

EDNA: Not now, Adele.

RICO: It's all right, Dell. Go on.

ALF [*Making another move*]: Check.

RICO: I moved already, Alf.

ALF: So did I, and I say "check" again.

ADELE: I was just going to open the box, Rico—

EDNA: Adele, I told you not to interrupt.

ADELE: But Rico just said—

EDNA: I don't care what Rico said.

ALF: Check! Check!

RICO: Now wait a minute. [*To* EDNA.] Who's playing this game, you or me?

EDNA: Just because Alfie's winning for once, you don't have to stop to listen to some silly story of Adele's about a man with the box your new vacuum cleaner—your new. . . . What was in that box, Rico?

RICO: What do you mean, what was in that box?

ADELE: But that was the weirdest thing of all I've been try-ing to tell you.

ALF: Rico, you're in check.

RICO: Wait a minute, Alf.

ALF: Wait a minute? I've been waiting all night for this.

RICO: Well, you can wait a minute longer, then. OK, Dell, your mother wants to know what was in the box. So tell us.

ADELE: But that was what was so weird. I was just going to open the box, when right behind me I heard this voice. "Hey, you!" And there was the man. *He'd* been hiding behind a parked car too! "What are you doing with that box?" he said. And he started toward me. Well, I wasn't going to wait till he got within reach of me. I ran. I just ran. I ran and I ran and I ran. I ran all the way to the coffee shop. So I never did see what was in the box.

EDNA: But it was your box.

ADELE: It certainly looked like it. What do you think, honey?

RICO: Dell, it wasn't our box. It doesn't make sense, see? It just wasn't our box. [*Turns back to game.*]

EDNA [*Beckoning her aside*]: Adele. What was there about it that made you think it was?

ADELE: Well, for one thing, when I was opening our box at home, I didn't do it very well, I guess, and I tore one of those flaps on top. Well, this box had the same flap torn.

RICO: Side flap or end flap?

ADELE: What?

RICO: Was the flap on the side or the end?

ALF: Forfeit!

RICO: Alf.

ALF: I'll give you three more minutes to get out of check, or you forfeit this game.

RICO: OK. [*To* ADELE]: Side or end?

ADELE: End.

RICO: Which end?

EDNA: Think, Adele.

ADELE: Well, with the writing where it said "Wonderwhirl Vacuum Cleaner" facing me, it was this end. Or maybe it was the other.

RICO: You see, you're not even sure which end it was. And besides, who doesn't tear a flap when they're opening a box like that? Everybody does. [*Turns back to game.*]

ADELE: There was the label, too. The "Handle with Care."

EDNA: What about it?

ADELE: It was crooked. I mean, I didn't notice it when I was unpacking our box, but as soon as I saw it on *that* box and the way it was stuck on crooked, I thought, "That looks familiar."

EDNA: Well, Rico. What about that?

ALF: Two minutes to forfeit.

RICO: All right, Alf. [*To Adele.*] So maybe it was our box. You threw it out, didn't you?

ADELE: I don't remember.

ALF: Sure you threw it out. He picked it up off the sidewalk.

ADELE: But why should he pick it up off the sidewalk and then throw it away again like that?

EDNA: Exactly.

RICO: Dell, how should I know? Maybe he's some kind of nut. Maybe he was just through with it. [*Turns back to game.*]

EDNA: And maybe he put it there on purpose, so somebody else could pick it up.

RICO: You watch too much TV, Edna.

EDNA: A drop, that's what they call it.

ADELE: He did sort of look like a criminal.

EDNA: You can't always tell by their looks, dear. It's actions that speak. Tell me, Adele, what was wrong with your old vacuum cleaner?

ADELE: Nothing, I guess. Rico got me the new one for a surprise.

EDNA: I see.

ALF: Don't just sit there, Rico. Move.

RICO: Take it easy, Alf. I'm thinking.

ALF: Well, can't you think a little faster?

EDNA: Of course, if the man was making a drop, someone would have to tell him where to make it.

ADELE: Golly, that's right.

EDNA: And before that, someone would have to tell him where to get it.

ADELE: Get the drop?

EDNA: Get the box. Someone who knew where there happened to be an empty vacuum cleaner box.

RICO: Dell, your coffee's getting cold.

EDNA: And after that, there'd have to be someone else to pick up the box and deliver it.

RICO: Dell?

EDNA: But it all comes back, Adele, to who knew where that empty box was.

RICO: OK, Edna. It all comes back to me, Dell, that's what she's trying to tell you.

EDNA: There isn't anyone else it could come back to.

ALF: Rico!

RICO: Look, Edna. You don't think Alf's playing chess on all those correspondence cards, do you? It's a code. He masterminds robberies from coast to coast on those cards. Been doing it for years.

ADELE [*Laughing*]: Honey!

EDNA: You can't get around me that way, Rico. Oh, I know it sounds silly to say you bought that vacuum cleaner just so you could have an empty box. But the sillier it sounds, the cleverer it is of you to do it. That's a well-known trick. And then getting us all out here on a night like this. I knew there was something fishy about that from the very beginning.

ADELE: Oh, come on, Mommy.

RICO: Getting you all out here? Well, I can see getting Dell away from the apartment so the guy could pick up the box. But why get you and Alf here too? Explain that, will you, Edna?

ALF: For God's sake, Rico, aren't you going to finish this game? You're still in check.

EDNA: He may never finish this game, Alfie.

ALF: I'll give you exactly four more minutes to forfeit.

EDNA: Why Alfie and me too? Because that's where the box is going. The first man gets it from your apartment and leaves it in the garbage can. The second man gets it from the garbage can, and, with the set of duplicate keys you've given him, takes it to our apartment. And when he gets to our apartment, he makes a phone call, and pretty soon a third man arrives. The second man gives him the box, and the third man pays for it and leaves. The second man waits a while, then he leaves, too. And then, he and the first man do the whole thing backwards with the money. [*Silence.*] Well?

RICO: You're not finished?

EDNA: I'm finished.

RICO: That's what I thought. [*Turns back to the game.*]

ALF: OK, Rico, let's see you get out of that.

EDNA: Wait, Alfie. I want an answer from him.

ALF: Answer? Answer to what?

EDNA: Haven't you been listening to what I've said?

ALF [*To* RICO]:   Move.

EDNA: I said, haven't you been listening to me, Alfie? [*Silence.*] Alfie, do you hear me?

ALF: Yes, I hear you. [*To* RICO.] Move.

EDNA: All right. Stay out of it, then, if that's what you want. Rico, are you going to answer me?

ADELE: Answer her, honey.

[*Silence.*]

EDNA: All right, then, Adele and I are going to our apartment.

RICO: Stay here, Dell.

EDNA: Oho. Stay here, he says. Ask him why, Adele.

RICO: Because I want her here. She's my wife, you know.

ADELE: Honey, please answer her.

EDNA: You don't want her to come with me because you're afraid when we get there, we'll find one of those hoodlums in our apartment.

ALF: Rico, will you move?

RICO: Now listen to me. Whatever was in that vacuum cleaner, lawnmower, lampshade box that Dell saw some bald-headed nut drop into an ashcan, I didn't put it there. I don't know where it came from, and as far as I'm concerned, it was going to the city dump. And furthermore, we are here to play chess because Alf and I like to play chess outdoors, in a public park, late at night, because there are *usually* no interruptions. And you are here because you're married to us.

EDNA: I'm not married to you, young man.

RICO: Look, Edna, you can stop trying to trump up something against me out of that silly-ass story of Dell's. You can't help Alfie win his game that way.

EDNA: Help Alfie win. . . . My Alfie doesn't need any help to win his games.

ALF: You're damn right I don't. And I'd just as lief not have any help in losing them either, Edna. Chess is a serious game. Frederick the Great played chess. You think he didn't take it seriously? Now you finish this game, Rico.

RICO: I'll finish this game, all right.

EDNA: Check him, Alfie.

ALF: He *is* checked.

RICO [*Moving*]:   Not any more, I'm not.

EDNA: Check him again.

ALF [*Moving*]:   I have! I have!

RICO [*Moving*]:   Have you?

[*The men study the board. After a moment,* EDNA *whispers something to* ADELE. *With a puzzled look,* ADELE *nods her head.* EDNA *sits back looking satisfied.*]

EDNA: How did you know he was bald, Rico? [*Silence.*] I said, Rico, how did you know that man with the box was bald?

RICO [*To* ADELE]:   Did I say that?

ADELE: You said, "some bald-headed nut." And he was.

RICO: Was he? It's just the way I saw him, Dell. Bald, stumpy legs, kind of fat. OK?

ADELE: But what about those other things?

RICO: What other things?

ADELE: The label and the tear and its being a Wonderwhirl box and what Mommy said about those three men.

RICO: She made it up, Dell. She made it all up.

ADELE: But I didn't make up what I *saw*, Rico.

RICO: Dell, who do you trust, me or her? [*Silence.*] Who do you trust, Dell?

ADELE: I don't know.

RICO: You don't know?

ADELE: I don't know who's telling the truth.

RICO: All right, then, *I'll* tell the truth. I'll tell you the truth. It's simple. It was our box. Yeah, our vacuum cleaner box.

EDNA: Aha!

RICO: I got Alf out here, that was easy. Got you two with us, that wasn't so easy, but I managed. And all so I could move the package. Very clever of you, Edna, to figure out that route. I've got to be careful of you next time. But right now those two men are in your apartment. Oh, they won't steal anything. Just make the deal and leave. But nobody's leaving here for another hour, understand?

ADELE: Rico!

RICO: I'll even tell you what was in that box. Yeah, I'll even tell you that. Christmas cookies! [*To* ALF:] Let's finish this game.

ALF: Now wait a minute. What do you mean, Christmas cookies? Is that the truth?

RICO: Sure it's the truth. And you're Frederick the Great.

EDNA: Alfie, are you going to stand for this?

ADELE: Rico, I'm sorry. I was being silly.

EDNA: *You're* sorry. After what he just did to you? He might as well have slapped you in the face, Adele. You may stand for that, but I'm not going to. Alfie, I repeat, are you going to let him slap your daughter in the face with a story like that, when he said he was going to tell her the truth?

ALF: No. No. I'm not. . . . Now, look here, Rico . . . I . . . I haven't been paying much attention to all this business about some kind of box and . . . and well, all that. But one thing I do know. Damn it, you can't talk to your wife the way you just did. Now . . . now you make amends.

ADELE: Honey, you don't have to. It was my fault.

EDNA: Stay out of this, Adele. Out. I'm going to have my satisfaction if I have to stay here all night. Isn't that right, Alfie?

ALF: Come on, Rico.

[*Silence.*]

EDNA: We're waiting.

RICO: You can wait till your tubes dry up!

ALF: Damn it, Rico, don't say that kind of thing to my wife!

RICO: I'll say any kind of thing I want. Now you listen to me, Alf. You want to play chess out here, we'll play chess. You want to turn this into a free-for-all, then I'll tell you something. You don't stand a chance against me. Look at the way you play that game. A ten-year-old kid could play better than that. You push me, Alf, and I'm warning you. I'll cut you down.

ALF: A ten-year-old kid! I'd like to see a ten-year-old kid use that Russian opening. I'd like to see a ten-year-old kid put you where you are on that board. You can't bluff me, Rico.

RICO: Bluff you, Alf? All right. Let me show you something. Come here, Edna.

ADELE: Honey, I was being silly about that box. I know you wouldn't do a thing like that.

RICO: Come on, Edna. Come here a minute. Where Alf can see you.

EDNA [*Moving to* ALF]: Alfie, aren't you going to do something? Aren't you going to make him apologize?

ADELE: He doesn't have to apologize.

EDNA: Not to you, Adele. To me.

ALF: I'll do something when I know what *he's* doing.

RICO: Thank you, Edna. That's just fine. A family picture. Now, look at her, Alf.

ALF: Oh for Chrissake, Rico.

RICO: No, look at her. Take a good look.

ALF: Rico, you just said something to my wife that you shouldn't have said. Now all you have to do is apologize. Come on, get it over with.

ADELE: Daddy's right, Rico. Oh, I know it's all my fault for not trusting you . . .

EDNA: Look at me, Alfie.

ADELE: But if you'll only say you're sorry for what you said to Mommy . . .

ALF: I'm not looking at you, Edna, just because he tells me to. That's playing into his hands.

EDNA: Then look at me because I'm asking you.

ADELE: If you'll only do that, Rico, I promise I'll never even think of not trusting you again. I promise.

ALF: I know what you look like, Edna. Now, you're the one that wants an apology, and I'm trying to get it. I don't have to look at you for that.

ADELE: Please, Rico?

RICO: Wish you could see her now, though, Alf. I'll bet that's just the way she looks at you every night, when you leave her alone at the dinner table.

ALF: Now, wait a minute.

RICO: Hurt and frustrated.

ALF: Now, wait a minute! If I don't happen to look at my wife, and . . . and what she looks like when she looks at me, is none of your goddamn business, Rico!

RICO: Oh, but it is, Alf. That's where you're wrong.

ADELE: Don't you hear me, Rico?

RICO: You want to see apples come into those cheeks, Alf, and a smile to those ruby lips? Yeah? Just watch. How about a little kiss, Edna? Want me to give you a nice little juicy kiss?

ADELE: Rico!

RICO: Come on, Edna. You know that's what you really want.

ALF: What the hell do you think you're doing?

RICO: Don't pay any attention to him. He's not paying any to you, you know.

ADELE: I just made you a promise, Rico. Isn't that enough?

RICO: Let's you and me go for a walk. To one of those benches, where it's nice and dark?

ALF: I'm warning you, Rico.

RICO: There's nobody around. We could really do it.

EDNA: Look at me, Alfie.

ALF: You go to hell!

RICO: See what I mean? Now's your chance, Edna.

ADELE: What more do you want from me, Rico?

RICO: Now's your chance to get it from sexy Rico, Edna. Isn't that what you've always wanted?

EDNA: Alfie, will you look at me?

RICO: I'm waiting, Edna.

ADELE: Don't I mean anything to you?

RICO: I'm waiting. Come on, baby.

ALF: Damn you, Rico!

RICO: He won't stop us.

EDNA: All right! Yes! Now you're going to look at me, Alfie. Now you're going to really look at me. [*She kisses* RICO.]

ALF [*Rising*]: You son of a bitch!

RICO [*Pushes* EDNA *away*]: I warned you, Alf.

ALF: But you can't do that!

RICO: I didn't do it to her, Alf. She did it to me. I wouldn't touch her again with a ten-foot barge pole. Kisses like a goddamn octopus.

EDNA: Alfie . . .

ALF: You stay away from me.

RICO: Hear that? Same old story, Edna. Stay away, stay away.

EDNA: I . . . I'm going for the police.

RICO: The police?

ALF: Goddamn it, Rico!

EDNA: I'm going to tell them about that box.

RICO: You've really lost your marbles, Edna. Look, forget

about that box. It'll take a hell of a lot more than a story like that from you to make trouble between me and Dell. Right, Dell? [ADELE *is silent.*] And as for you, Alf—

ADELE: Rico, that's enough.

RICO: What?

ADELE: Oh, Rico.

RICO: What's got into you?

ADELE: What's got into me? Oh, Rico, you've always been so sure of me.

RICO: Dell.

ADELE: Yes, you have. It's like . . . it's just like one of those TV shows where they get someone up from the audience. Yes, and as soon as they only have the person's name and what they do—like housewife—the master of ceremonies is so sure of who that person is and what he's going to make her do—

RICO: For Chrissake, Dell.

ADELE: That it's like it doesn't matter any more who she really is. That master of ceremonies tells her who she is. And even though she maybe makes some little personal remark, he just kids her along till she runs out of things to say. And then she gives up. Oh, they always give up. . . . You always kid me along when I make some little personal remark, Rico. You did that as soon as you started to take me out. And after a while, I gave up, too. I ran out of things to say. I let you decide who I was. And then I married you.

RICO: Dell, you don't think I meant it when I kissed Edna?

ADELE: You're just like that master of ceremonies, Rico. You don't care what you do—not even to me—so long as it keeps you ahead of everybody else. You'll do anything!

RICO: Dell!

ADELE: Leave me alone. [*She exits. Silence.*]

RICO [*To* EDNA]: God damn you!

EDNA: Me? You brought that on yourself.

RICO: The hell I did! If you hadn't started with that story . . .

ALF [*Starting to go*]:   I'll catch up with Adele.

RICO: That's right, Alf. You run away. Just keep running away.

ALF: I'll ask her to stay with us.

RICO: The hell you will!

ALF: She'll stay as long as she wants.

RICO: She spends one night with you, and she's not coming back to me.

ALF: That's for her to decide.

RICO: That's for me to decide.

ALF: Not any more, Rico. Not any more.

RICO: Oh?

ALF: You're not deciding anything any more. It's out of your hands. Oh, you can *decide* all you want, but nobody's going to pay you any attention. I'll see to that.

EDNA [*Anxious*]:   Alfie.

RICO: I won't hurt him.

ALF: Damn right you won't. I don't know how you fooled me as long as you did. When I think of all the times I've sat down . . . But that's not the point. I never should've let you into my house, that's the point.

RICO [*Quietly*]:   Finish this game, Alf?

ALF: What?

RICO: You want to finish this one last game?

ALF: You're damn right I do. [*Goes to chess table.*]

EDNA: What about Adele?

ALF: You catch up with Adele. [RICO *sits.*] Now I'll show you a thing or two.

[*The two men begin to play.* EDNA *withdraws upstage. Neither man is aware of her presence.* ALF *plays with a new assurance,* RICO *with a new concentration. The game moves quickly.*]

ALF: Check.

[RICO *moves out of check.* ALF *moves.*]

RICO [*Moving*]:   Check.

ALF [*Moving out of check*]:   It's not that easy, my boy.

RICO [*Moving*]:   Check.

[*For the first time,* ALF *hesitates before moving.* RICO *is play-ing to kill now, and* ALF *has begun to realize it.* ALF *moves out of check,* RICO *moves, then* ALF *takes a piece.*]

ALF: Hah.

RICO [*Moving*]:   Check.

[*From now on,* ALF'S *game disintegrates rapidly. When he moves out of check,* RICO *takes a piece.*]

RICO: Your knight. [ALF *moves,* RICO *takes a piece.*] Your bishop. [ALF *moves again.* RICO *takes another piece.*] Your rook. [ALF *moves.*] And checkmate. [ALF *is stunned.* RICO *rises.*] Too bad, Alf. [*Starts out, but pauses when he sees* EDNA.] If Dell's at your house tonight, tell her I'll be over to get her in the morning. [RICO *exits. A long pause. Then* EDNA *comes downstage.*]

EDNA: Alfie?

ALF [*Looking up*]:   You still here? Why don't you go home? [*Looks back at board.*]

EDNA: Alfie, I . . . [ALF *brings his fist down hard on the chess table.*] Alfie.

ALF: Only hadn't got my knight. If that son of a bitch only hadn't taken my knight.

[*A pause, and then* EDNA *sits beside him on the bench.*]

EDNA: What did he take it with?

ALF: Queen.

EDNA: Couldn't you have taken one of his pieces?

ALF: That's when I checked him. He had me then.

EDNA: Oh. Show me, Alfie.

ALF: You really want to see?

EDNA: Yes.

ALF: All right. Wait'll I get the men. [*Starts putting chess-men back on the board.*] My king was here. My queen's bishop here. I had a couple of pawns. He had his queen . . . [*Fin-ishes setting up the pieces.*] There. Now, when I checked him with my bishop, I was counting on losing the bishop—draw-ing him into a trap—and then moving in with that pawn. What I didn't see was, that made my rook vulnerable. Now if I'd moved my rook instead . . . [EDNA *stifles a yawn.*] I'll show you some other time.

EDNA: No, show me now, Alfie. I . . . I'm sorry. If you'd moved your rook . . . where? Where would you have moved your rook?

ALF: I'd have moved it . . . moved it . . . I don't know where I would have moved it.

EDNA [*Moving the piece*]:   What about there?

ALF: There? . . . Well . . . well, yes, and then. Then he'd have to move his queen! And then, by God, I'd have had him! I'd have mopped up the board!

EDNA: Yes, Alfie, you'd have won. [*Stifles another yawn.*]

ALF: Just let me put these away, and then we're going home. [*Putting chessmen in box.*] Think Adele will be there?

EDNA: She might be.

ALF: Think she'll go back in the morning?

EDNA: That's for her to decide, Alfie.

ALF [*With authority*]:   That's right. That's for her to decide. [*He is ready to go; takes* EDNA *by the arm; they start out.*] Tell you what, Edna. I'll show you that Russian opening tomorrow.

EDNA: My blanket, Alfie. [*Goes to bench, picks up blanket, folds it, and rejoins* ALF.]

ALF: It's a real beauty. Puts the other player on the defensive right away.

[*They exit.*]

CURTAIN

Upstairs Sleeping

Harvey Perr

FOR GEORGE AND GRACE

". . . It's not only the corn that needs strong roots, you know,
it's us too. But what've we got? Go on, tell me, what've we got?
We don't know where we push up from and we don't bother
neither. . . ."

—*Arnold Wesker*

THE TIME: *Spring, 1950*

SCENE: *The kitchen of Esther's house, Brooklyn.*

People in the Play:
ESTHER
SAM, her husband
FRIEDA, her daughter
SEYMOUR, her grandson

The curtain comes up on a cluttered, dirty kitchen. Most prominent among the room's furniture and assorted bric-a-brac is a sink filled with dirty dishes at stage right, which is next to a closed window, the vision of which is clouded; a table with three chairs at stage center—there is a radio on the table; a stove and a cot at stage left. On the wall directly behind the cot is a clock.

    ESTHER, *65 years old, is standing at the sink as if she were about to wash the dishes, her head in the direction of the window.* SAM, *70 years old and an invalid, is propped up on the cot.*

ESTHER: I'll have to wash this window one of these days. The sun don't come through anymore. Was a time, Sam, when you could look out and see the plant on the windowsill green, growing. Remember, Sam?

SAM: Yes, Esther.

ESTHER: What do you mean, you remember? Did you ever have time to look out the window? . . . [*Begins to wash the dishes.*] Look at how they pile up. We don't even eat that much. And the dirt ring around the sink. What was the name of that stuff they advertise on television, supposed to make your sink white as new? Remember, Sam?

SAM: I don't remember. . . .

ESTHER: Look who I'm asking. Put the television on and you're fast asleep. . . . [*She sits down, forgetting the dishes, in a slump, and wearily faces the audience; she turns to look at the clock behind* SAM.] What time is it, Sam?

SAM: About nine o'clock.

ESTHER: What do you mean, nine o'clock? Why don't you look at the clock? It's only eight-thirty. . . . Where's Seymour, Sam?

79

SAM: Upstairs!

ESTHER: Upstairs? How do you know, you were upstairs?
. . . I don't know. I never saw a boy, he doesn't see his mother
in a year, and when she comes home, he sleeps. Kids today,
they don't care. Was a time, Sam, when a son cared. Remember, Sam?

SAM: Yes. When a son . . .

ESTHER: It's like talking to a stone. You and your grandson.
Like talking to a stone. . . . He's upstairs? What is he doing?

SAM: Sleeping!

ESTHER: What do you know? Because a boy is in his room,
it means he's sleeping? Sleep, that's all he's good for! So he's
in his room . . . upstairs . . . sleeping. Was a time, Sam,
when you could look out and see the plant on the windowsill
green, growing. When it didn't take a million years for a half-
hour to go by. When a son cared for his mother. Remember,
Sam?

SAM: Yes, Esther.

ESTHER: What do you mean, you remember? How can you
remember? It was so long ago! . . . You want coffee? I just
put it up!

SAM: I'd like a cup of coffee. If it's fresh.

ESTHER: You'll have to wait. It's not ready yet! [*She remains
seated.*] I wanted the place should be clean when Frieda comes
home. Just look at this mess! Sit and wait for someone and a
half-hour seems like a million years. But try to do something
Saturday and you no sooner turn around it's Sunday! Look
at the window. It's so dirty, you can't even see what it's like
outside. If it's raining or if the sun is shining! Put on the
radio, Sam, and we'll see what the weather's like.

SAM: I can't reach . . .

ESTHER [*She puts the radio on*]:   What can you do? Nothing! [*Music blares forth from the radio.*] What kind of music
is that? That's music? Just noise. Was a time when music was
music, not noise. [*She gets up to pour the coffee.*] One sugar
or two?

SAM: Two.

ESTHER: You know the doctor said only one sugar.

SAM: All right, one!

ESTHER: Make up your mind, one or two. [*She puts two sugars in his coffee.*]

SAM: One.

ESTHER: Too late. I already put two. [*She gives him the coffee.*] Is it good?

SAM: Very good, Esther.

ESTHER: Thank God, I still make good coffee. Is it strong enough?

SAM: Yes.

ESTHER: It's not so strong today!

SAM: It's good coffee.

ESTHER: What do you know about coffee? To you, a cup of coffee is a cup of coffee. It's good?

SAM: Yes.

ESTHER: Good! [*Pause.*] Where's Seymour?

SAM: Upstairs!

ESTHER: I know he's upstairs. What's he doing?

SAM: I don't know.

ESTHER: I'll tell you what he's doing. He's sleeping, that's what he's doing. Nothing bothers him. You and Seymour. Nothing bothers you. Light heads! Do for you, slave for you! Do you show appreciation? What's the use of talking? Was a time when you did something, it was appreciated. Remember, Sam?

SAM: Yes, Esther.

ESTHER: What do you know? You appreciated? [*Pause.*] What time is it?

SAM: About nine o'clock.

ESTHER: It's not nine o'clock yet. Frieda should be here already. She said on the telephone she'd be here nine o'clock. So where is she? You want another cup of coffee?

SAM: No, Esther.

ESTHER: I thought you liked it.

SAM: I did. It's good coffee.

ESTHER: Then have another cup.

SAM: Okay.

ESTHER [*She pours another cup*]: How much coffee do you think I made? Save some for Frieda. Here! [*She gives him the cup of coffee.*] Good?

SAM: Good!

ESTHER: Good. [*Pause.*] I think I'll wake Seymour up.

SAM: Let him sleep.

ESTHER: Why?

SAM: He came in late.

ESTHER: How do you know, you heard him?

SAM: No.

ESTHER: So how do you know it was late? A boy knows his mother is coming and he comes in late. What kind of a son is that? Was a time when a son cared for his mother. [*Doorbell rings.*] What was that?

SAM: The door.

ESTHER: How do you know? It sounds like the telephone.

SAM: Maybe it's the telephone.

ESTHER: How could it be the telephone? Who calls so early? It's the door. It must be Frieda. I'll go. [*Exits.*]

FRIEDA [*Offstage*]: You got two dollars, Mom? I only have a twenty. The cabby don't have change.

ESTHER [*Offstage*]: Sure. Here. [*She comes back into the kitchen.*] How do you like that? No hello. Just give her. [FRIEDA, *40 years old, in a mink coat, enters with a suitcase.*]

FRIEDA: Hi, Mom. [*Kisses her.*] How are you, Papa? [*Kisses him.*] God, when was the last time you brushed your teeth? [*Pause.*] Well, here I am! Back home again. Can't you say anything? How do you like my new coat? Real mink, like it?

ESTHER: It's beautiful. When did you get it?

FRIEDA: About a month ago. Like it, Papa?

ESTHER: What does he know about mink? I can tell, it's a good piece of fur. How much did it cost?

FRIEDA: What's the difference? It's mink, ain't it? That's all
that counts.

ESTHER: There's mink and there's mink.

FRIEDA: This is good mink.

ESTHER: I can see it's good mink, but you don't know till you
know how much it costs.

FRIEDA: Money! That's all you think of. Well, it cost Charley two thousand bucks.

ESTHER: Two thousand bucks? Some mink!

SAM: So much money for a coat?

ESTHER: What do you know about mink? [To FRIEDA:] So,
how is Charley? And Norman?

FRIEDA: Everyone is fine. You know.

ESTHER: I'll bet you didn't get any sleep. All night on the
plane.

FRIEDA: I slept.

ESTHER: You slept?

FRIEDA: Sure.

ESTHER: You're telling the truth? Because I know you, you
don't sleep on a plane.

SAM: She said that she . . .

ESTHER: Who's asking you? I know my daughter, she doesn't
sleep. [To FRIEDA:] So you slept? All the way?

FRIEDA: Well, not all the way.

ESTHER: What'd I tell you? I know you, Frieda, you can't
sleep on a plane. So how is Charley? And Norman?

FRIEDA: Fine, everyone's fine.

ESTHER: Norman's a big boy now, I bet.

FRIEDA: Six years old.

ESTHER: He must be a big boy. Who does he take after?

FRIEDA: I don't know. He's so smart.

ESTHER: Well, he doesn't take after Charley.

SAM: Why do you say that? Charley is very nice. . . .

ESTHER: Frieda knows what I'm talking about. Charley is
smart, when it comes to making money.

FRIEDA: That's so bad?

ESTHER: Who says it's bad? But there's smart and there's smart.

FRIEDA: Don't worry about Charley!

ESTHER: You want a cup of coffee? Freshly made.

FRIEDA: Just what I need. A good cup of strong coffee.

ESTHER [*She pours the coffee*]:   It's plenty strong. One sugar or two?

FRIEDA: No sugar.

ESTHER: No sugar? Cream?

FRIEDA: No, black.

ESTHER: Black?

FRIEDA: Black.

ESTHER: Since when do you drink black coffee?

FRIEDA: I always drink black coffee.

ESTHER: Do you think I remember? Was a time when I remembered how you took your coffee. [*She gives the coffee to* FRIEDA.] Is it good?

FRIEDA: Delicious.

ESTHER: Thank God I still make a good cup of coffee. . . . How's the weather outside?

FRIEDA: Sunny.

ESTHER: Nice?

FRIEDA: Very nice. Of course, in Miami, it's ten times as warm.

ESTHER: In Miami, that's a different story. It's sunny outside? It doesn't look like rain?

FRIEDA: No, Mama.

ESTHER: In here, you can't tell. The window is so dirty it always looks like rain.

FRIEDA: It won't rain.

ESTHER: That's nice. It's sunny. Did you hear that, Sam?

SAM: I heard, Esther.

ESTHER: How come? You never listen to me.

FRIEDA: Oh, Mama, remember Elsie Bloom?

ESTHER: The beautician.

FRIEDA: She sells wallpaper.

ESTHER: Blonde hair.

FRIEDA: Redhead.

ESTHER: Her husband is a salesman.

FRIEDA: A bookie.

ESTHER: Tall.

FRIEDA: Short.

ESTHER: Two kids.

FRIEDA: One.

ESTHER: A daughter.

FRIEDA: A son.

ESTHER: Sure I know Elsie Bloom. What about her?

FRIEDA: What I was going to say is her son, remember he played the piano so good? Well, her son Neil, only eighteen years old mind you, sings on television now. He makes five thousand dollars a week.

ESTHER: Some kid. He always was talented.

FRIEDA: Well, anyway, Elsie and her husband don't have to pick up a finger to do a thing.

ESTHER: Sure, with a kid like that. Some kid. What does he do, play the piano?

FRIEDA: He sings.

ESTHER: Some kid. He always was talented. Sings, too!

FRIEDA: Eighteen years old.

ESTHER: Five thousand dollars a week!

SAM: And Seymour? You're not proud?

FRIEDA: Who says? Where is Seymour?

ESTHER: Upstairs.

FRIEDA: What's he doing upstairs?

ESTHER: Sleeping.

FRIEDA: Sleeping?

ESTHER: Sleeping!

FRIEDA: At nine o'clock?

ESTHER: At nine o'clock. At ten o'clock.

SAM: He's a good boy. He goes to school.

ESTHER: What do you know? He sleeps. All day, he sleeps. Just stays in his room and sleeps.

FRIEDA: See what I mean? Neil Bloom, eighteen years old, he's making five thousand dollars a week, his family doesn't worry for nothing. Get my point? And my son sits in his room up there and plays with himself.

ESTHER: That's how you talk about your son? A boy who goes to college. Was a time when a mother cared for a son.

SAM: A good boy like Seymour.

ESTHER: What are you talking about? From good and bad, you know the difference?

FRIEDA: He knew I was coming home, no? So where is he? [She calls to him.] Seymour darling, your mother's here. Come on down. Are you up yet, Seymour?

ESTHER: They don't care anymore. That's the trouble with the world. Nobody cares.

FRIEDA: Look at this window. It's so dirty you can't see out.

ESTHER: I've been meaning to clean that window. But every time you start something these days, there's no time to finish. It's that damn television. You put it on and you're through for the night. It's that damn television. That's the trouble with everything. The damn television! Was a time, Frieda, when you could finish what you started.

FRIEDA: How are you managing here?

ESTHER: Between Papa's pension and my sewing and the five dollars you send every week . . .

FRIEDA: I wish I could send more, Mama, but you know . . .

ESTHER: Between Papa's pension and my sewing and the five dollars you send every week, we manage. Was a time when we managed better. Remember, Sam?

SAM: Yes, Esther.

ESTHER: You remember! What do you remember? We never had it so good. The mortgage paid, a television, no struggling! Listen to him! I'm telling you, Frieda, we never had it so good. Only one thing. Nobody comes anymore. Was a time when this house was always filled with people. When you made fresh coffee for people and it was appreciated. Remember, Sam?

SAM: Yes, Esther.

ESTHER: Sure, you remember! You and your Communist friends, always striking, never holding a decent job. Did any of you work? No, you'd just sit here and talk while good-natured Esther slaved to feed you and to make coffee. Thank God there's prosperity in this country and there's no more Communists. Thank God for one thing. That there's no more lazy loafers in my kitchen talking about Marx and Lenin and Peace on Earth.

FRIEDA: Yeah, Papa! Where's the peace on earth? Where's the white knight you used to tell me about when you put me to sleep? Where, Papa?

ESTHER: White knights yet! The kind of dreams fathers stuff into the heads of their kids! White knights on white horses, when outside the sky is black with fog and a man can't get a decent job. White knights? Ask him, Frieda. Ask him where is the white knight.

[*During the following monologue,* FRIEDA *unzips her dress, wiggles out of it, removes her stocking garters from her girdle, lets the stockings fall, removes the shoes and stockings, and, at the end, is left a ludicrous figure in a slip, a mink coat, and bare feet.*]

FRIEDA: Why ask? So what if the white knight is fat and greasy. As long as he makes a living. As long as he supports you and your kids. You've got money in the bank, a fur coat on your back, and a diamond ring on your finger, and as long as it's all real, that's all that counts. Sure, you want something better out of life, but you learn. You learn to take what you can get. What are we, privileged characters? We take. And we settle for what we get. It's not so bad. It could be worse. I got money in the bank, a fur coat on my back, a diamond ring on my finger. And it's all real. That's all that counts. It's all real!

ESTHER: You're sure the sun is shining?

FRIEDA: I'm sure.

ESTHER: It's not going to rain?

FRIEDA: Positive.

ESTHER: From here you can't tell if it's sunny or if it's raining.

FRIEDA: It's sunny.

ESTHER: This window is so dirty, you can't see what it's like outside.

FRIEDA: Where's Seymour?

ESTHER: Upstairs.

FRIEDA: What does he do all day, in his room?

ESTHER: Sleeps!

SAM: He's a good boy!

ESTHER·   To you, everyone, everything is good. What do you know? I ll go wake him up. [*She exits screaming:*] Seymour! Seymour!

[*During the following scene,* FRIEDA, *still in her mink coat, removes her nail polish, while seated at the table.* SAM *half-sings, half-chants a Yiddish song, of how old he has become. Without understanding the exact meaning of the song, we should feel the muffled pain of this man.*]

SAM:

> *Kinder yorn, zisse kinder yorn,*
> *Eybig bleibt ir vach in mein zikor'n;*
> *Ven ich tracht fun ei'yer tseit,*
> *Vert mir azoy bang un leid,*
> *Oy, vi shnel bin ich shoyn alt gevorn.*

> *Kinder yorn ch-hob eich ongevoyrn,*
> *Mein getrei'ye mamen oych farloyrn,*
> *Fun der shtub nishto keyn flek,*
> *Feygele is oych avek,*
> *Oy, vi shnel bin ich shoyn alt gevorn.*

FRIEDA: So tell me, Papa. Where is the white knight? Where is the tree that grows in Brooklyn?

[SEYMOUR *appears, in his pajamas, ruffled, heavily bearded, tall—as a tree, if you like—and he doesn't say a word.*]

FRIEDA: Well, aren't you going to give your mother a kiss, you haven't seen her in a year? [SEYMOUR *crosses to kiss her.*] God, when was the last time you used deodorant under your arms? [ESTHER *enters.*] So hairy! Just like his father! When was the last time you saw your father?

ESTHER: Last week he went.

FRIEDA: Last week?

ESTHER: Sunday.

FRIEDA: You saw your father?

ESTHER: Last week.

FRIEDA: When last week?

ESTHER: Sunday.

FRIEDA: Sunday?

SAM: Good morning, Seymour.

[SEYMOUR *kisses his grandfather.*]

FRIEDA: So how is he?

ESTHER: Ask him. It's like talking to a stone.

FRIEDA: How is he?

SEYMOUR: Who?

FRIEDA: Your father.

SEYMOUR: Oh, my father. I saw him last week.

FRIEDA: When?

ESTHER: Sunday!

FRIEDA: Last Sunday?

SEYMOUR: What last Sunday?

ESTHER: You saw your father.

SEYMOUR: I know.

ESTHER: You want coffee? It's fresh.

SAM: It's good coffee.

FRIEDA: Look how tall he is! I can't get over it.

ESTHER: You want coffee, yes or no?

SEYMOUR: I'll take.

ESTHER: Butterfingers is going to pour his own coffee. Hurray!

FRIEDA: So tall, just like his father. How is he? What do you talk about?

ESTHER: To a stone, what can you talk about? The coffee, it's good?

SEYMOUR: Like mud.

ESTHER: What do you know about coffee? Give him instant coffee, give him. That's the trouble with the world. Everything is instant. Was a time when a person had time to make coffee, to taste coffee, to know about coffee.

FRIEDA: He asked for me?

SEYMOUR: What's it like outside?

ESTHER: Sunny.

SEYMOUR: How can you tell? This window is so dirty.

FRIEDA: Not even a word?

SEYMOUR: The radio said rain.

ESTHER: There, what'd I tell you? I knew it was going to rain.

FRIEDA: One word?

SEYMOUR: Why don't you wash this window?

FRIEDA: What do you talk about? Answer me!

ESTHER: That's all I have to do? Wash windows?

SEYMOUR: And the dishes. This place is filthy.

FRIEDA: Talk to me. I'm your mother. Tell me.

ESTHER: All day he sleeps in his room . . . upstairs . . . and he tells me to wash windows. Do you know what I do all day?

SEYMOUR: You make coffee that tastes like mud.

ESTHER: I cook, I sew, I take care . . .

SAM: Esther . . .

ESTHER: Shut up. Can't you see I'm talking?

SEYMOUR: Why don't you let him speak?

ESTHER: Did he ever say anything worthwhile?

SEYMOUR: For God's sake, let him talk!

[SEYMOUR's *urgent tone startles* ESTHER *and* FRIEDA *into turning to look at* SAM, *who is finally given a chance to speak. For a long moment,* SAM *stares ahead, blank-faced and stunned.*]

SAM: I . . . I just . . . what I wanted . . . I mean . . . I can't . . . Seymour, I can't!

ESTHER: Look at him. Could he ever do anything?

SEYMOUR: Shut up! [*To* SAM:] Try. Please. What is it you want to say?

SAM: I can't . . . Seymour, I can't . . .

SEYMOUR: You can't what?

SAM: Can't speak . . . can't breathe. . . . Trapped . . . locked . . . locked . . . locked . . . in a cage, Seymour! . . . I can't breathe. . . . Let me out . . . Seymour, find a way . . .

SEYMOUR: The dirty bastards!

SAM: Don't Seymour. . . . No good, that's no good. . . . Not the way . . . Seymour, I can't . . . I can't!

SEYMOUR: Tell me.

SAM: Trapped. . . . My throat, Seymour . . . I can't breathe. . . . Open the window, please!

[SEYMOUR *crosses to open the window.*]

ESTHER: Don't open the window!

[*The window is opened.*]

SEYMOUR: Why? What are you keeping out? The sun?

ESTHER: My plant!

SEYMOUR [*He is holding the plant*]:   It's dead. Covered with little black bugs!

ESTHER [*She takes the plant from* SEYMOUR]:   Was a time when you could look out and see the plant green, growing.

FRIEDA: Tell me, Seymour. What do you talk about, you and your father? Talk to me.

SEYMOUR: Things.

FRIEDA: What things?

SEYMOUR: Just things!

FRIEDA: About . . . about me, Seymour? [FRIEDA *is pleading now, on her knees.*]

SEYMOUR: Sometimes. Your coat's getting dirty. It's on the floor, Mom.

ESTHER: Was a time when it didn't take a million years for a half-hour to go by. Remember, Sam?

[*The action freezes.* ESTHER *stares abstractedly out the win-*

dow, the plant in her hand; SAM *looks out into the audience, one hand at his throat, the other hanging limply at the side of the cot;* FRIEDA *is on her knees, her mink coat trailing on the floor.*]

CURTAIN

In A Cold Hotel
Ben Maddow

People in the Play:

SALAMO (GERALD HOFFMEYER WATKINS)
SOLDIER, his son
GIRL

Curtain rises. At first, all is darkness, in the obscure midst of which someone is snuffling and snoring. The light slowly increases.

It's a fairly large corner room on the third floor of a de-cayed hotel, in a city of fifty thousand or so on the Eastern Seaboard. There is winter sunlight outside, but the dark green roller shades have been drawn against it. The two windows in the room look out in two directions.

By this comparatively dim light, one can see four huge objects; three of them are steamer trunks, on which the word SALAMO *has been stencilled in white paint; but the fourth is a bed with brass fittings, in which a headless co-coon of quilts continues to snore like a pump on the verge of exhaustion.*

Suddenly, outside and down below, the sound of a brass band. They play three-fourths of the first stanza of "My Country 'Tis of Thee," but break off in the middle, almost directly under the windows, leaving a whole musical phrase maddeningly unfinished.

At this desecration, the cocoon of quilts explodes, and a man in a night shirt hurls himself out of bed. He slaps one of the shades with his fist. It rolls up with a violent noise, admitting a blaze of daylight into the room. There's lug-gage everywhere, old-fashioned, with brass locks and corner plates, and stencilled in white: SALAMO.

Muttering and cursing, he yanks up the stubborn win-dow. An icy breeze enters the room. Clutching his night shirt together, he yells down three stories to the street. He is SALAMO *himself; he has a strange flat nose, with huge dark nostrils, and broad bones in his cheeks, a real show-business face.*

95

SALAMO: Finish the tune!—You blasted [*Making it up.*]—sons of Huns!—Ha, ha! Play!—Play. If you've got any breath left. [*Pretending to be the band:*] Papapah! ! Papapah! [*To himself:*] Great God in the morning! It's cold! [SALAMO *shivers, slams down the window, hurls himself back into bed.*]

[*Three floors below, sound of the invisible brass band, blaring, disjointed, with one off-key trumpet. It picks up the patriotic tune and plays it from the beginning with furious gusto. Now the hall door opens about two inches. Sound of a knock, repeated twice, but too timidly to be heard over the band. The door is pushed open all the way, the band finishes in a grand sour chord, and the visitor enters the room unnoticed. He's a young SOLDIER, wearing the long overcoat, campaign hat, and bandage puttees of World War I. He's tall, splendidly built, sunburned, brawny, with knitted scarf and gloves and pale blue eyes. He's also more or less ugly, but is entirely unaware of this fact.*]

SOLDIER [*Softly*]: Papa—?

[SALAMO *snores on. The* SOLDIER *clears the chair of a live white pigeon, and sits down. Pause. He begins to whistle.* SALAMO *sits up at once in his nest of quilts, and stares at the intruder.*]

SOLDIER: Yessiree.

SALAMO: Yessiree? Yessiree what? I haven't said anything yet, have I?

SOLDIER: Nothing I care to repeat, nossir.

[*He puts his hand forward and touches, very gently, a black silk opera hat on one of the trunks. A bowl of flowers springs forth in full bloom. The* SOLDIER *is partly scared, partly delighted.* SALAMO *stands up out of bed, a quilt draped around him.*]

SALAMO [*Shouting*]: Were you raised in a stable?

SOLDIER [*Quietly*]: Nossir. I was raised in a two-story shingle house—with a painted porch front and back.

SALAMO: Fascinating. Did it have any doors?

SOLDIER: Oh, yessir! Several.

SALAMO: Then go and shut 'em before I freeze to death.

[*The boy goes back and closes the door.*] Now open 'em again, and get out.

SOLDIER: Oh, I can't possibly do that, sir.

SALAMO [*Coming closer*]:   Why not?

SOLDIER: I ain't decided to tell you yet.

SALAMO: Tell me what? [*Coming still closer.*] You're in the wrong room, soldier boy. And I'm the wrong sex.

SOLDIER [*With sympathy*]:   You're hairy, ain't you, sir? And you look ridiculous.

[SALAMO *recoils.*]

SALAMO: What the devil did you expect? You woke me up before breakfast.

SOLDIER [*Politely*]:   You're a liar, sir. I saw you at the window, bawling out the brass band.

SALAMO: What's your rank, soldier?

SOLDIER: Private First Class. Which is funny. There ain't anything too first-class about it. And there certainly ain't anything private.

SALAMO: Can you handle a machine gun?

SOLDIER: Nossir. I'm a specialist, sir.

SALAMO: In what?

SOLDIER [*Imaginary shovel*]:   Military sanitation.

SALAMO: How did you get tabbed with that dubious distinction?

SOLDIER [*Still shoveling*]:   I tooken a test, sir, and the results were ninety-nine point eight. I think they had it confused with my temperature.

SALAMO [*Putting both hands on the boy's shoulders*]:   Boy, disregard it! Drop your tools and grab a bayonet! Go over the top and get me a couple of Huns! And take off those puttees! You expect to kill the Kaiser in those puttees?

SOLDIER: I don't expect to kill anybody whatsover.

SALAMO: Where's your patriotism, boy?

SOLDIER: I been troubled by that, sir.

SALAMO: Where's your guts?

SOLDIER: Right here, sir.

SALAMO: Where's your good old-fashioned American get-up-and-go?

SOLDIER: Don't talk against my mother, sir.

SALAMO: I don't know your mother from a five-and-dime whore.

SOLDIER: I believe you do—Papa.

SALAMO [*Aghast*]:   Papa!

SOLDIER: Papa.

[SALAMO *retreats toward his bed, fishes behind him under the pillow, and retrieves a pint bottle of some amber fluid.*]

SALAMO: Papa—?

SOLDIER: Papa. [SALAMO *pours himself a slug directly from the bottle, and gasps, groans, and wipes his lips. The* SOLDIER *goes and gets a tumbler off the top of the littered dresser.*] Is this glass sanitary, Papa?

SALAMO: I haven't used it yet, if that's what you mean.

[*The* SOLDIER *takes the bottle from* SALAMO *and pours himself half a glass.*]

SOLDIER: What is it, Papa?

SALAMO: Applejack—[*The boy fills up the rest of his glass.*] —diluted with aromatic spirits of country skunk. [*The* SOLDIER *drinks it down.*] Have a little more. A little more helps to kill the taste. [*The* SOLDIER *obliges; he has another half glass of applejack.*] Feeling sick?

SOLDIER: No sir.

SALAMO: Not even a faint touch of mental paralysis?

SOLDIER: No sir.

SALAMO: What have you got for a stomach, a cast-iron Franklin stove?

SOLDIER: It's a gift, Papa. I can digest anything whatever.

SALAMO: Not like me.

SOLDIER: In no way like you, Papa. I wish I was.

[SALAMO *goes and lifts the boy's face with one hand, examining it carefully, as though it were a piece of china.*]

SALAMO: Papa?

SOLDIER: Papa—Does that surprise you, sir?

SALAMO: No, not at all—There are parts of the United States where I could not throw a stone from a local train—without hitting one of my romantic moments.

SOLDIER: Except—I'm not a romantic moment, Papa. I'm strictly legal.

SALAMO: How would you know a disgusting thing like that?

SOLDIER: I saw the birth certificate.

SALAMO: What was the name on this criminal document?

SOLDIER: It was yours, sir. Gerald Hoffmeyer Watkins.

SALAMO: Don't tell me my name! I know my name! What was her name?

SOLDIER: Maggie Roberts.

SALAMO [Curiously]: Maggie Roberts, Maggie Roberts, Maggie Roberts—! Oh, glory God, Maggie Roberts! [With emotion.] You're the only son I ever had with malice aforethought. I wanted to punish that woman—! Maggie Roberts—ach! [Softly.] How old are you, boy?

SOLDIER: Nineteen years old. The fifteenth of January. They say I had an exceptionally big head of hair.

SALAMO: Congratulations.

SOLDIER: Why did you abandon me, sir?

SALAMO: Abandon? Who abandoned who? [Emotion overcomes him; he goes over to the bed, sits, and begins to dress.] Son, I tried to see you a thousand times. Every time my circuit passed through Davenport, Iowa, I tried to track you down. You were never there, nor that dratted woman, either. Where the devil were you?

SOLDIER: Listening to the player pianna, I guess. Mama would hear you were in town, she'd see the posters and all, and she'd take me and my sister, and hide us until you were gone—in The Gold Star Moving Picture Palace.

SALAMO [With slobbering contempt]: "Palace—Palace"—!

SOLDIER: Don't you like moving pictures, sir?

SALAMO: I have never, drunk or sober, set foot in a place where they debase humanity by flattening actors into two dimensions. [SALAMO *begins to dress: white socks, white shoes, black trousers, white shirt, white collar, and white collar button.*]

SOLDIER: Know something? When I go to moving pictures, I don't take notice of the actors. There's too many other things going on. Suspense. Intrigue. Biff! Bang! Wham! Throw the body down the old abandoned mine! You know what I mean? Why, I can't hardly bear to wait until next week. Episode Nine. Don't fail to miss it. Some of these foreigners with mustaches have suspended him—

SALAMO: Him, who him?

SOLDIER: Harry Houdini. Over a vat of boiling acid—in the umbrella factory—

SALAMO: Harry Houdini—suspended? I don't hardly believe it.

SOLDIER: Suspended, Papa! That's a fact!

SALAMO: They should open their fingers—and drop him.

SOLDIER: Why, Papa?

SALAMO: Because—Harry Houdini is a traitor!—You won't believe this, but that man has gone so far as to write a book. *How To Deceive Your Friends.* Imagine!—Selling the secrets of the profession for a dollar-fifty in hard covers!

SOLDIER: A dollar-fifty buys a lot of green apples.

SALAMO: I'm not that fond of green apples, why are you that fond of green apples? Don't you believe in heredity?

SOLDIER: Nossir. I believe in the stars, sir.

SALAMO: The stars—never did a thing for me. Except add to the general confusion.

SOLDIER: The stars impel—they do not compel.

SALAMO: I hope, for your sake, you didn't make that up.

SOLDIER: Do you believe in the stars, Papa?

SALAMO: Do I have any choice?

SOLDIER: The stars control our destiny, Papa. Don't you b'lieve that, Papa?

SALAMO: When you get my age, you believe nothing and nobody.

SOLDIER: That's awful, Papa! I got to get a Bible and straighten you out.

SALAMO [*Mock sarcasm*]:   I like you, son!—What's your true name?

SOLDIER: Same as yours. Gerald Hoffmeyer Watkins.

SALAMO: Gerald Hoffmeyer Watkins!—I want to ask you this, Gerald Hoffmeyer Watkins. Did she ever mention me to you?

SOLDIER: Upon occasion, sir.

SALAMO: What did she say?

SOLDIER: Well, sir, she described you to be a handsome, nice-mannered bum.

SALAMO [*Harshly*]:   That's true! We were two of a kind. [*He puts his head in his hands.*] Maggie Roberts! She never told a lie in her life. Except one: and that was a whopper— How's your sister Caroline?

SOLDIER: She's fine, sir, just fine! She'd be proud you remembered her name.

SALAMO: And Maggie? How's old Maggie?

[*The* SOLDIER *comes close, and helps his father put the back stud into his collar.*]

SOLDIER: You know something? [*Softly.*] She's died, Papa.

SALAMO [*Very quietly*]:   Died?—Finished?

SOLDIER: Yes, Papa.

SALAMO: When?

SOLDIER: Last year, Papa. The tenth of July.

[SALAMO *walks about the room, and begins to strike the walls with his right fist.*]

SALAMO: Died? Before me? Died? Died? I never thought that would happen.—Died, she wasn't that old, son!—She had hair the color of red velvet—How did it happen?—No, don't tell me—All death is nasty—The details, how I hate the details!—[*Bitterly, almost violently.*] "What kind of a coffin would you prefer for the dear departed? We have the Deluxe for thirty-seven cash."

[*The* SOLDIER *treads on a woman's slipper. He picks it up and dusts it off, examining the pink pompom over the instep.*]

SOLDIER: She died going up the stairs in the old house. Heart trouble. The delayed consequence of double pneumonia— You know the stairs in the old house?

SALAMO: I was never there, son—I was the dirty part of her life.

SOLDIER: You're not as bad as she made out.

SALAMO: Think so?

SOLDIER: You perform magic, don't you?

SALAMO: Soldier boy, there's no such thing.

SOLDIER: You take a silk hat, and bring forth a bird, a bunny, a glass of pink champagne, don't you?

SALAMO: A cheap trick, soldier boy!

SOLDIER: You bring pleasure to the whole world, Papa.

SALAMO: So does a scarlet woman of the streets!

SOLDIER [*Mildly*]:   I don't cast no stones, Papa. [*He hands the feminine article back to his father.*]

SALAMO: Well, God bless you. [SALAMO *goes and embraces his son, who stands rather stiffly.* SALAMO *wipes a tear from the corner of each eye. The tears are both real and rhetorical. He points to one of the trunks.*] Like to see part of my act, son?

SOLDIER: I'd be proud and pleased.

[SALAMO *goes to the opposite wall. He knocks several times.*]

SALAMO: Girl! Girl! [*There is a snarl of feminine rage from behind the wall.* SALAMO *now beats at the exposed plumbing, violently.*] Come on out here, girl! The U. S. Army awaits you! On the double!

[*The hall door is shoved open, but the* GIRL *is invisible behind it.*]

GIRL [*Offstage*]:   Go 'way. You're a dirty old man!

SALAMO: I resent just one of those adjectives—I don't have time for both.

GIRL [*Offstage*]:   I hate you, Mr. Watkins, from the bottom of my heart!

[*The* SOLDIER *takes the slipper back from his father and hands it through the open door.*]

SOLDIER: Is this your slipper, miss?

GIRL: That's only one of them. Where's the other? I bought those in Pittsburgh—and goddam it to hell—!

SOLDIER: I'll look for it, ma'am. May I?

[*The* GIRL *walks slowly into the room. She's dressed in a long skirt and a frilly white blouse, and her dark hair is piled up in a great mass on top of her head. She has a sullen, stupid, yet intensively sensitive face, and she stares at the* SOLDIER *from head to toe. It makes him warm.*]

GIRL: Well, well!—Who are you?

SOLDIER: I'm one of his sons, ma'am—Are you one of his daughters?

SALAMO: My God! I sincerely hope not.

GIRL: He's not just whistling "Dixie."

SALAMO: Would you mind? Getting in the trunk? I want to show my boy how it's done.

GIRL: How what's done, and to whom? [*Without pause.*] I don't know if he's old enough.

SOLDIER: I got to be pretty soon. I'm going to Paris, France, in two weeks.

GIRL [*Coming to look straight into his eyes*]:   There's a Paris, Pennsylvania. Did you know that?

SOLDIER: Why, no! Is that a geographical fact?

GIRL [*One hand on his uniform*]:   And a Paris, Michigan—Also a Paris, Wyoming.

SOLDIER: Ain't that something?

GIRL: So there's no need to go all the way to Paris, France—

SALAMO [*Coming between them*]:   Leave the kid alone!—And get in the trunk, before I send you back to the five and dime. Where I found you.

GIRL [*Into the boy's eyes*]:   Don't believe him, soldier boy. There was articles there which retailed for twenty-five and even thirty-five cents.

SOLDIER: I believe that!

GIRL: And furthermore, soldier boy, I can go straight back to 47th Street, and get into toe-shoe ballet, which was just dying to have me!

SALAMO: Ballet? Ballet! On those feet?

GIRL [*Shouting by now*]:   They loved my feet! The manager told me so! He did!

SALAMO [*Shouting, too*]:   What else did that greasy little manager tell you?

[*The GIRL begins to weep; she turns away from the two men, her shoulders shaking with huge sobs.*]

SOLDIER: Oh, gosh, don't cry, please don't cry!

SALAMO: She's· not crying! She's doing a scene! She's an actress, not a woman! She's practicing in real life what she might be called upon to perform—on stage! [*Turning to the girl.*] All rightie, you can quit now! And—[*Pointing.*]—get into the trunk, before I lose my temper!

GIRL: No!

SOLDIER: Oh, please. Please do.

GIRL: I won't do a damn thing without my costume.

SALAMO: Well, get into your costume!

GIRL: My costume—is downstairs getting laundered. You spilled ketchup all over it last night. Don't you even re-member?

SOLDIER: Exactly how—did he get—ketchup—?

GIRL: I think you'd rather not know.

SOLDIER: You're right. I admire you for that.

GIRL [*Firmly*]:   I love you, soldier. I wish there were one mil-lion of you. Wherever I roam.

SOLDIER: There is. That's the hell of it.

GIRL: Poor soldier. Here I go, coming between a boy and his dad. I'm mean, I'm evil, and I'm ignorant.

SOLDIER: Don't believe that for one little minute.

GIRL: Would you like to see my trick with the trunk?

SOLDIER: I surely would.

GIRL [*To SALAMO*]:   I'm doing it for his sake, not for yours.

[*The* GIRL *opens the trunk, gets in, closes the lid. A second later, her feet pop out of the bottom, fully clad in black net. At the other end of the trunk, her face appears, smiling up at the* SOLDIER.]

SOLDIER [*Applauding*]:   Wonderful!—Wonderful!

GIRL: I haven't done nothing, yet. The monster is going to cut me in half—

[SALAMO *advances with a carpenter's saw, which he brandishes in the air.*]

SOLDIER: Papa. I don't think I care to watch—

SALAMO: Of course not! That's the point! It's repulsive. To the nth degree! It's universal! Intellectual! Enormous! Vibrant! Static electricity!—And it brings out the doctor in all of us. [*He bends the saw, making it sing and hum. As if to an audience:*] Ordinary crosscut saw. Bought it half an hour ago. In a hardware store right down the street. Seventy-five cents. I was overcharged. [SALAMO *begins to saw through the middle of the trunk. The sawdust spills from the crack.*]

SOLDIER: It's beautiful, Papa! Just a beautiful, beautiful trick!

GIRL [*Sulking in the trunk*]:   I think your papa wishes it were real.

SALAMO: I think the only time you find it hurts, is when it cuts through the spine. [*The* GIRL *utters a horrible, unearthly scream.*] Please! Please! Don't improvise!

GIRL: I hate you from the bottom of my soul.

SALAMO: Prettiest bottom I ever saw.

SOLDIER [*To the* GIRL]:   Is this wicked old gentleman an acquaintance of yours?

[SALAMO *still saws madly away.*]

GIRL: He'd like to be! Oh, he'd like to be! He's just spoiling out of his mind to be my friend!

SOLDIER: Ain't he too old?

GIRL: No. He's not! Which is unfortunate!

[SALAMO *pauses, as if hurt or insulted. He pulls out the saw, wipes it, and with the same cloth, wipes the sweat from his brow.*]

SALAMO: This trunk—soldier boy—is how I met your mother
—Maggie Roberts! Oh, Maggie Dolores Roberts!

GIRL [*From the trunk*]:   Do tell!

SALAMO: It was the Proctor Theatre. In Davenport, Iowa.
Big house, ten-piece orchestra. Fiddles—za-za-zoom. I step
forward. I have them put a baby spot on to the audience, and
I ask for volunteers—

SOLDIER: Papa—?

SALAMO: She stepped up! [*Seizing hold of his son by both
lapels.*] A fine, big woman, peace to her soul! Maggie Roberts by name!

SOLDIER: I know. But Pa—

SALAMO: She come up fourteen steps to the stage, and she
fitted this trunk like a hand in a glove, and I took her to Span-
ner's Restaurant next door—

SOLDIER: Please—Papa—!

SALAMO: Infatuation! She wrote my name on the lampshade.
Enclosed in a heart. When we ended in Davenport, she run
away with me. Packed her trunks and run away with me—

SOLDIER: Took my sister along with her.

SALAMO: Two steamer trunks full of shirts and middy
blouses.

SOLDIER: She told me you tricked her.

SALAMO: Maybe I did. I'm no fool. But from that moment
on, she outfoxed me a thousand ways. [*He begins to saw away
again, deeper and deeper through the trunk.*] We were on
the road ten months or maybe eleven, when your mother—
zippo!—disappears in the dead of winter. Comes back with a
man. It took me five mad minutes 'fore I saw his collar was
on backwards. Minister of the Gospel. Man by the oddball
name of Reverend Lovett—!

SOLDIER: Papa—?

SALAMO: Two days later, while I was recovering from this
hasty marriage—she took the two of you—

SOLDIER: Me and sister Caroline?

SALAMO: —and wrapped you up real good—and ran back to Davenport by the morning train. I never saw her again.

SOLDIER: But, Papa?

SALAMO: What, boy?

SOLDIER: Why didn't you follow after her?

SALAMO: Pride. Pride.

SOLDIER: Didn't she love you?

SALAMO: She left me a note on the top of this trunk. It said, "Goodbye, you ten-cent Casanova!" It broke my heart.

SOLDIER: But she loved you, didn't she?

SALAMO: Half of her did. I don't know which half.

SOLDIER: Didn't you love her, Papa?—Well—didn't you?

SALAMO: Son, there's degrees and qualifications to love.

SOLDIER [*Suddenly, passionately*]:   No, there ain't! [SALAMO *goes to the mirror and studies his left lower canine.*] Papa— what about this girl right here?—Do you love her? Or do you not?

SALAMO [*To the girl*]:   You want me to lie?

GIRL [*It takes her a long moment to decide*]:   No. I guess not.

SALAMO: Well, then, I am in love. Passionately, devotedly! And I'll tell you the name of the person involved—[*Pointing at himself in mirror.*] It's him! I love that stupid man from the bottom of my soul! [*Beginning to comb his hair.*] I've got a lifelong attachment to that old crum, my boy! If he dies—I die! What about that, eh? What about that, son? [*He hurls down the comb and walks to the hall door.*]

GIRL [*From the trunk*]:   Where you going?

SALAMO: For a long, long walk.

GIRL: To hell, I hope.

SALAMO: I wish I was. In this class of hotel, hell is a lot closer than the bathroom. [*He pulls a towel off the dresser and goes out. He reappears at once, stares at each of them, then goes out again, shutting the door with a bang. The* SOLDIER *and the* GIRL *are alone.*]

GIRL [*To the* SOLDIER]:   You going to bring me my supper, or you going to let me out? [*The* SOLDIER *opens the trunk, and the* GIRL *gets out. Bent at the knees, she pretends to be unable to straighten out. She stumps around the room.*] You've got a pretty uniform. I love olive drab.

SOLDIER: Well, thank you very much.

GIRL: Papa begets boy, Papa loses boy, boy loses Papa. Don't be so cheerful. He may be back.

SOLDIER: I won't be here.

[*She gets to her feet.*]

GIRL: Wait! Please wait.

SOLDIER: Why?

GIRL: I don't know.

SOLDIER: He's horrible. Why do you stay with him?

GIRL [*Turning*]: It's a job.

SOLDIER: That's not what I mean.

GIRL [*Turning and dancing*]: Last week he borrowed a two-dollar bill off me.

SOLDIER: And never paid it back?—I know.

GIRL [*Still turning*]: You don't know. It's much worse than that.

SOLDIER: What could possibly be worse than welching on a two-dollar bill?

GIRL [*She stops*]: He took my money and bought me a two-dollar box of candy. It brought tears to my eyes! Sincerely!

SOLDIER: He won't trick me.

GIRL: He will. He will.

SOLDIER: He won't! You'll see! I'm tougher than he is. I got my mama's character. Stupid, but stubborn. I'm going to walk out of here and down to the Erie Railroad Station and into the front line so fast—!

GIRL: Wait—wait—please wait.

SOLDIER: Why? He don't have one ounce of feeling.

GIRL [*Touching him*]: Wait—and say goodbye to him.

SOLDIER [*Moved*]: My sister Caroline has hair like yours— What are your feelings toward my dad?

GIRL: What are yours?

SOLDIER: I don't know yet. But by gee, I'm going to find out. [*The door opens beyond them, admitting* SALAMO *again.*]

SALAMO [*To the* GIRL]: Go and get me some hot coffee— with a cup around it.

SOLDIER [*To the* GIRL]: Go on. Do what he says. [*He pitches her a coin.*] Go on—go! [*The* GIRL *leaves, walking backward, looking from father to son. The* SOLDIER *shuts the door, shutting her out. He turns.*] And you, too!—Go on—[*To the invisible audience:*] It's over! It's all there is! The act is over. Go on home! Go on, get out! [*Turning to* SALAMO.] They won't go, Papa. We've got 'em fascinated. [*As if in a fury, the* SOLDIER *begins to open one drawer after the other. He pulls out pieces and contraptions of the various tricks. At last he finds three colored balls, and begins to juggle them in the air.* SALAMO *watches, sweating and yet smiling.*]

SALAMO: Where the devil did you learn to do that?

SOLDIER [*Juggling*]: A-watching of you.

SALAMO: You caught my act? When?

SOLDIER [*Still juggling*]: I've been at every performance since I came in by train last Tuesday afternoon.

[SALAMO *begins, grimly, to join the juggling act. Father and son toss the colored balls from one to the other.*]

SALAMO: You were there at the Wednesday matinee?

SOLDIER: Yes.

SALAMO: Saturday matinee?

SOLDIER: Yes.

SALAMO: Thursday night, when I dropped the box on her foot?

SOLDIER: You threw it. You didn't drop it—I saw you!

SALAMO: All right—you saw me—! You saw me! [*With great emphasis, but quietly.*] What did you think of my act? The truth, now!

SOLDIER: Papa, your—act—stinks—on—ice.

SALAMO: That's what I need—constructive criticism. [*He collects all three juggling balls, opens the window, and hurls them out into the snow.*]

SOLDIER: I tell you what you need, Papa. What you need, Papa, is a smashing climax.

SALAMO: Such as what?

SOLDIER: Such as this. [*He reaches in his pants pocket, draws out a two-foot length of chain.*]

SALAMO: What's that?

SOLDIER: Harry Houdini.

SALAMO: Queer, ain't it? Looks like a bicycle chain to me. But I could be wrong.

SOLDIER: Harry Houdini! Harry Houdini can bust it in three minutes flat! Three minutes of excruciating suspense—!

SALAMO: Give it here!

[*The* SOLDIER *tosses the chain to his father.*]

SOLDIER: Loop it twice around each hand.

[SALAMO *does so, pulls the length of chain apart across his fists, straining violently. His face sweats, the veins bulge in his neck.*]

SALAMO: It's real.

SOLDIER: Yes, Papa, it's real. [*The* SOLDIER *watches, intently.* SALAMO *bends double in the effort to tear apart the chain with his hands.* SOLDIER *says at last:*] Papa, quit. [*Becomes more apprehensive.*] Papa, please—you'll tear your heart wide open—Now, Pa, I don't want you to hurt yourself!—Papa, please—please, please! [*He goes over and pulls the chain out of his father's hand.* SALAMO *gasps, sits down on the edge of the bed, lies back gasping. The* SOLDIER *hurls the chain away across the room.*] I can't do it, either, Papa. [*Suddenly, still panting, still sweating,* SALAMO *crosses to one of the unopened trunks, pulls it open, draws from it a pair of very large steel scissors.*] What's the matter, Papa?

SALAMO: Come here, Son. Here, give me your trigger finger!

SOLDIER: What?

SALAMO: Gimme it here! I can make a cripple out of you in ten seconds flat.

SOLDIER: Papa! Now you're acting cuckoo!

SALAMO: I was never more sincere in my life. I've got one son, do I want him murdered? Those Huns have got high explosive shells, which, boom! And turn what was recently a man—into raspberry jelly. [*His son tries to wrestle the shears away from him. His father won't let him touch the weapon.*] We're fragile, Son, extremely fragile. I mean, the human race! One morning, you wake up, the earth smells of new-mown hay. No, it's not new-mown hay, it's poison gas. Fifty thousand years of slow civilization, and what's in the culmination of it all? Poison gas! [*He pretends to gasp and choke.*] Don't do it, Son. Don't go to war. Leave that madness to the rest of the world. The decent, clean, hard-working, stiff-collar boys! The kids in the balcony! You and me, Son, we're too dirty to go to war. Besides—I need a partner! Come with me. Come with me, Son! We'll have good times together. I'll show you the world. Not the way you think it is. But the way it is—the way it really is! [*He takes the shears in two hands, and bends it double. It's made of painted rubber.*] There's nothing in the whole wide world that's sincerely genuine.

SOLDIER: I sincerely disagree, Papa.

SALAMO: Fine, I like an argument. Stimulates the brain, like fish. I'll even compromise with you, and improve the act. Buy the chain bit from Houdini. Dry-clean the costumes, regardless of expense. And give you equal billing up there along with me. Will you do it? You'll do it! You got to do it!

SOLDIER: Papa, I'm in the Army!

SALAMO: Give 'em notice!

SOLDIER: I can't.

SALAMO: Why, are you afraid of Woodrow Wilson?

SOLDIER: I'm afraid of you, that's all I'm afraid of, Papa!

[*A knock at the door.*]

SALAMO: Stay out! I'm dressing! [*But the* GIRL *reenters, carrying a steaming cup, a napkin, and a spoon. She hands the three articles to* SALAMO. *She stirs the cup with the spoon for him.*] What are all these lumps?

GIRL: Noodle soup.

SALAMO: What are you trying to do, nourish me? [*But he eats it, noisily. Slurping his soup:*] He's turned us down, girl.

SOLDIER: What do you want? I can't desert! It took me nine and a half months to where I could put on a uniform without itching to death!

SALAMO: Nineteen years of age, and already the boy has turned sensible. It's sad. When I was nineteen, Son, I tore a piece out of the world and ate it for breakfast. But what did you eat? Rural flapjacks and sweet Iowa butter. Take a look at you! Hup, hup, trip, fuh! You don't have a button that ain't shined up like a star in the sky.

SOLDIER: Papa—don't run down the stars. They're important.

SALAMO: The stars! Ha! Ever swim in the Ohio River by night? And float on your back and look up at those stars?

SOLDIER: No, Papa.

SALAMO: There's no hup, hup, trip, fuh, up there. It's all wildness. Those stars drink applejack together and make love in the sight of God eternal—

GIRL: Oh, shut up! Shut up!—There's more to life than making love—!

SALAMO: That's true. And that's sad, girl. [SALAMO *sits down on the bed, as though he were now completely exhausted.*]

SOLDIER [*Quietly, but in considerable agony of spirit*]: Papa —Papa. We don't think alike, Papa!—Look, I had a paper route when I was seven. Rain, shine, or snow. In the winter I used to wrap up the newspapers in wax paper, and throw 'em low so as not to break off the icicles on the porch! I wanted to be wild, Papa, but I didn't know how. Could you have taught me different? If you were there?

SALAMO: I was never there. Or anyplace else.

SOLDIER: Papa. I've got one hour left, Papa. The train leaves at three o'clock sharp. You hear me, Papa?

SALAMO: Yes. Three o'clock sharp.

SOLDIER: Want to walk with me to the station?

SALAMO: Station? What station?

SOLDIER: Erie Railroad Station.

SALAMO: Don't believe I will, Son.

SOLDIER: Well, then—so long, Papa—It was nice to talk to you, Papa!

SALAMO: Son—?

SOLDIER: Papa?

SALAMO: Take care of yourself.

SOLDIER: You know me, Papa.

SALAMO: And, Son—

SOLDIER: Yessir?

SALAMO [*Routinely*]: Catch the Kaiser for me, soldier boy. Bring him home in a chicken-wire cage.

SOLDIER: Not me, Papa. You've got the wrong son.

SALAMO: You write letters home?

SOLDIER: Every Sunday morning.

SALAMO: Send my regards.

SOLDIER: Maybe. I'll think about it.

SALAMO: To sister Caroline.

SOLDIER [*Violently*]: I said, maybe! They hate the mention of your name. [*The* SOLDIER *goes to the door, and opens it. Quietly, now.*] Want to come along, girl? Snow smells good. I'll buy you a couple of beers. And pig's knuckles. You like pig's knuckles? I mean the green-sour-apple kind. [*The* GIRL *looks toward him, then looks at* SALAMO, *then back to the* SOLDIER.] Well, pretty girl? [*The* GIRL *shakes her head in negation.*] Well, girlie, see you around. [*The* SOLDIER *puts out his hand to the* GIRL; *she puts his palm for a second against her cheek. The* SOLDIER *goes out, closing the door firmly. As he does so,* SALAMO *leans back in the bed, against the disordered pillow, and points to the wall.*]

SALAMO: Just look here, girl—no, here, at this wall. Chaps too lazy to lean out of bed, have snuffed out their cigarettes on this wall—Now, ain't that the saddest thing you ever saw? Ain't it, girl?

GIRL: No.

SALAMO: Show you what kind of a hotel, there's a sink in

the hall, with a sign over it. Big letters: NOTICE! THIS
IS A SINK!

GIRL [*Softly, as she begins to put the room in order*]:   That
was no way to say goodbye, Mr. Watkins. It was awful. Awful.

SALAMO [*Coarsely*]:   What did you want me to do? Kiss his
behind?

GIRL: You don't mean that.

SALAMO: I don't mean anything.

[*The* GIRL *has passed by one of the windows, and now she
looks down toward the street.*]

GIRL: He's coming down the steps of the hotel. Ooh, he
walks so straight. Ooh, he's so handsome.

SALAMO: From that angle, anybody's handsome.

GIRL: Wave to him. He's looking up here! [*But* SALAMO *remains on the bed.*] Oh, please! He might die and you might
never see him again—

SALAMO: No!

GIRL: He's gone, he's turned the corner and gone.

SALAMO: Why didn't you go with him?

GIRL: I won't tell you.

SALAMO: I want you to go.

GIRL: Well, I won't!

SALAMO: What's holding you here? Why do you stick with
me?

GIRL: My back salary, that's all!

SALAMO [*Fiercely*]:   Listen, girlie. You know something? I
lock the door every Thursday at twelve. Have you noticed?
Twelve noon—and dye my hair in the dirty sink of some cold
hotel, wherever we happen to be. The natural color of my
hair—is smudge white! Color of old snow—where they sprinkle
salt upon it, and melt it down the gutter—! Why didn't you
go with him? Why stick with me? What's the reason?

GIRL: I don't want to tell you!

SALAMO: Girlie! Nothing I do is human. I've known a million women and don't remember more than ten or twelve.
That's a lie, too. I don't remember any of them. All I re-

member is the doors closed, and the sweat, and the rain. And the shadow on the wall. And they must have been such marvelous women—gorgeous! Beyond compare! Every one of them had something wrong with them! Ears too big! Or their hair like manila string! Or sick in the chest! Or unhappy with their miserable husbands! Or choked up inside! Or wild nerves!—Or some darn screw loose in their heads!—I've lived a life of careless love—by picking on cripples!

GIRL: What kind of cripple am I?

SALAMO: I'm the cripple. I been cold all winter. Cold. Cold as a corpse. There's never heat in these cement hotels! And it's three and a half miles to the nearest can! And the furnace goes out regular—between eight and six. They've got a man special for that—to put out the furnace.

GIRL: What kind of a cripple, please!

SALAMO: The truth is I hated to see my son leave this room. It give me ice around my heart.

GIRL: What kind of a cripple, Mr. Watkins!

[SALAMO *takes her two hands and holds them in his.*]

SALAMO: You really want to know?

GIRL [*Softly*]:   Tell me, what kind of a cripple?

[SALAMO *lifts her hands and kisses them.*]

GIRL: What kind of a cripple?

SALAMO: You're sad. You're just terribly sad. That's all is the matter with you.

GIRL: Say you love me, will you? Or don't—no—don't!

SALAMO: Stay, girlie. You'll have a grand old time. Honest.

GIRL: Grand.

SALAMO: Girlie! It's a great year. We got bookings clear up into Ogden, Utah.

GIRL: Oh, grand—isn't that just grand?

SALAMO: Ever fall in love with a full-blood Indian, girlie?

GIRL: Grand! Grand!

SALAMO: There're real live Indians on the street in Ogden. Ugh! Ugh! How! How!

GIRL: If I'm sad—you make me sad.

SALAMO: I know that, girlie. But don't leave me—for a trivial reason like that.

GIRL: Why did you treat your son that way? I can't forgive you. At least—march him to the troop train—

SALAMO: No! I was sick of him! I wanted him to go.

GIRL: I don't believe it.

SALAMO: I wanted him out of my sight.

GIRL: Why? I don't understand you any more.

SALAMO: Because if he'd stayed here one more minute, I'd have spoiled his life forever!

GIRL: How? By kissing him goodbye?

SALAMO: By the truth, by the awful, exact truth!—I'd have spilled my guts and told him the truth.

GIRL: What truth?—What truth!

SALAMO: That his pretty sister Caroline—

GIRL: The one with curly hair?

SALAMO: Curly like yours—Yes. That his sister Caroline—is not his sister—but his mother.

GIRL: Oh, God—no! You seduced her?

SALAMO: I loved her.

GIRL: What kind of a cripple was she?

SALAMO: She was age twelve and a half.

GIRL: And so—you didn't tell him.

SALAMO: I didn't tell him. I didn't want him to think worse of me than he does.

GIRL: I think—that was a good deed.

SALAMO: "In a naughty world."

GIRL: Don't make fun of yourself! It was good, it was good!

SALAMO: Was it really?

GIRL: It was, really.

SALAMO [*Almost weeping*]:   Oh, God, this is a wonderful country! America! U.S.A.! Grand! Just grand!—And it gets colder every year, girlie.

GIRL: Does it, though?

SALAMO: When I was young, we used to have summers where we have winters, and vicey-versey.

GIRL: "Was it, really?"

SALAMO: "It was, really."

GIRL: But I mean, really!

SALAMO: I don't know, little girl. I lost my twenty-year calendar. Really.

GIRL: Is it going to snow right now, do you think?

SALAMO: No. Not now. Not yet. Later, maybe. When it's dark. When all the couples in all of northern New Jersey and parts of Pennsylvania—have gone to bed.

GIRL: You think, ever in this world, I'll make you happy?

SALAMO: Girlie, girlie!—Don't go marching off to war.

GIRL: I have never had no such intention, Mr. Watkins.

SALAMO: Let the Kaiser live to a ripe old age, girlie!

GIRL: All right. I will.

SALAMO: And get me a cup of genuine coffee, will you?

GIRL: I don't know about that. But I'll try. [*She goes and opens the door and then stands there, pressing her forehead against the panel of the door.*]

SALAMO: What's the matter now?

GIRL: Oh, nothing—I love you, that's all. I don't know why! —Can you tell me why?

SALAMO: It's the stars, girlie. The stars. [*He opens the window and begins to do deep breathing exercises.*] The ignorance of the stars.

[*The GIRL goes out, looking back at him fondly.*]

CURTAIN

The Nine O'Clock Mail

Howard Sackler

THE SCENE: *The suburban living room of* TED *and* CYNTHIA.

People in the Play:

TED
PHYLLIS, his daughter
CYNTHIA, his wife
PETER
POSTMAN

Built into the door, upstage, is a brass mail slot, very highly polished.

TED *sits at a card table loaded with paper, envelopes, letter openers, sheets of stamps, a small scale, pens, pencils, etc. Under the table are two large wastebaskets filled to overflowing. He taps the table nervously, stares at it, looks at his wristwatch, then impulsively seizes an envelope, addresses it, folds a sheet of notepaper, inserts it, seals the envelope.*

His little girl PHYLLIS *enters, hatted and coated and carrying her schoolbag.*

TED: Off to school, Phyllis?

PHYLLIS: Yes, Daddy. [*Comes closer.*] Aren't you going to work today?

TED: Don't know yet, sweetie. Maybe later on. I don't feel too hot this morning.

PHYLLIS: Ah, what's the matter? Should I go tell Mommy?

TED: No, no thanks. Better just run along.

PHYLLIS [*Peering at the envelope*]: Who are you writing to, Daddy?

TED [*Flipping it over quickly*]: Whom, Phyllis.

PHYLLIS: Whom.

TED: Yes. No one important, dear.

PHYLLIS: You write so many letters now.

TED: Well, the more you send the more they send you, honey.

PHYLLIS: Oh wow, Daddy, you get more mail than anybody.

TED: I do all right, I guess—hey, nearly half-past!

PHYLLIS: OK. I'm going. [*Pecks him on the cheek.*] Can I say you're coming to the parents' meeting, Daddy?

TED: What parents' meeting?

PHYLLIS: Tomorrow, Daddy. I told you! Miss Gunn says it's not just the mothers, and the fathers are supposed to come too this time.

TED: Is that so?

PHYLLIS: I told you yesterday, Daddy!

TED: Yes, but you're only a kid. Why didn't they *write* to the parents about it?

PHYLLIS: Didn't you believe me?

TED: Of course I believed you, honey. But they should send out a letter for something like this. It's quite a large school, they have the facilities—typists, mimeograph machines—

PHYLLIS: But it's just our class, Daddy, not the whole school—

TED: Then Miss Gunn should have written invitations herself, and put them in the mail. [*Mutters.*] Big deal, two or three dozen letters.

PHYLLIS: Daddy—

TED: Look, I don't pay taxes so that you can be some sort of messenger girl, Phyllis.

PHYLLIS: So I'll say you can't come?

TED: No, you tell Miss Gunn I'd be delighted to come, but I'd appreciate a little note about it first—what time, what room—

PHYLLIS: It's in Room—

TED: Uh-uh! No messenger girlie, Phyllis!

PHYLLIS: Daddy, you wouldn't get the letter in *time*—

TED: Special Delivery! Easy! She posts it as late as she likes tonight, and I get it first thing in the A.M. tomorrow. Here— [*Tearing off a row of stamps.*] Five, ten, fifteen, twenty times two—give her these, honey. After all, we shouldn't impose—

PHYLLIS [*Not taking the stamps*]:   Ah, Daddy, come on. It's Room 2—

TED: Phyllis, take the stamps and go to school.

PHYLLIS: I forgot what I'm supposed to say.

TED: No, you didn't! You're ashamed to ask her, aren't you?

PHYLLIS: Well, nobody else's father—

[*A click at the door slot, something comes through.*]

TED [*Leaping to the door*]: What's that?

PHYLLIS: Mail.

TED [*Grabbing it and throwing it down*]: No, just the damned newspaper! The first mail won't come for another 10 minutes. Please take the stamps, Phyllis.

PHYLLIS: Ah, Daddy—

TED: Be a good girl, honey—

PHYLLIS: You said I shouldn't be a messenger girl, Daddy.

TED: Now you're being fresh.

PHYLLIS: It'll look funny, Daddy—

TED: Oh, I see! You want to be exactly like everyone else there! That's what they teach you, huh? [*Holds out the stamps to her.*] Well, we're putting a stop to that right now—

PHYLLIS: Daddy, please! I'm going to miss the school bus!

TED: Take these and tell her I must have that letter!

PHYLLIS: You're making me late!

TED: I'll give you a quarter, Phyllis . . .

PHYLLIS: I don't want a quarter. . . . [*She weeps.* CYNTHIA *enters, carrying a dish towel; she wears no makeup and her head is bound in a kerchief.*]

CYNTHIA: Goodness, what's wrong!

TED: She's very disobedient.

PHYLLIS: Daddy wants me to make Miss Gunn write him a letter.

CYNTHIA: Oh, no.

PHYLLIS: Special Delivery!

TED: Is that so terrible? I'm supplying the postage.

CYNTHIA: Go to school, Phyllis. [*Hugs her.*]

TED: That's it, spoil her, let her get away with murder.

PHYLLIS [*Kissing* CYNTHIA]: Goodbye, Mommy.

TED: No kiss for Daddy, eh?

PHYLLIS: Goodbye, Daddy. [*Kisses him.*] You're not mad at me? Promise?

TED: No, honey. Have a nice day. And if you pass the mailman—

PHYLLIS [*On the run*]:   I know, Daddy—ask him to please hurry up. [*Exit.*]

TED: She was all ready to give in, Cynthia. I wish you'd take my side for a change.

CYNTHIA: We shouldn't involve Phyllis in this, Ted.

TED: Gunn would have sent it, you know. It was a cinch! She couldn't get out of it once she had the stamps.

CYNTHIA: That's true, Ted, but—

TED: OK, sweetheart. You're right. I'm sorry. [*Glances at his watch.*] He'll be along soon, anyway.

CYNTHIA: You're going to wait?

TED: Yes.

CYNTHIA: It's . . . 8:40, Ted.

TED: I know, I know. But I have to get the mail.

CYNTHIA: Well . . . how about some coffee while you're waiting?

TED: No thanks, honey.

CYNTHIA: Ted . . . will you be going in to the office . . . afterwards?

TED: And miss the 2:30 mail?

CYNTHIA: I could ring you the second it arrives, Ted . . .

TED: Sweetie—

CYNTHIA: You could have an early lunch and then—

TED: Maybe tomorrow, sweetie. It's a great idea, but really, I don't feel so hot.

CYNTHIA: What is it—stomach?

TED: Well, nothing specific. You know. Besides, I think there's a registered coming later.

CYNTHIA: Ted, I could sign for that.

TED: Do I get in your way here, Cynthia? Is that it?

CYNTHIA: Oh darling, not at all—

TED: Truth? I can wait for it out in the garage—

CYNTHIA: Sweetheart—

TED: No, I mean it. And look, I'm not being a martyr. I'll bring the electric heater out there—

CYNTHIA: Don't be silly, Ted.

TED [*As she dusts*]: Can I help you with anything?

CYNTHIA: No thanks. Not just now.

TED: Oh . . . Cynthia.

CYNTHIA: What, Ted?

TED: You're worried, aren't you?

CYNTHIA: Well . . .

TED: Truth!

CYNTHIA: Yes, I am, a bit.

TED: About the job!

CYNTHIA: Yes, about that, and—

TED: Say, I'll make a deal with you!

CYNTHIA: What do you mean?

TED: If there's a good 2:30 I'll go in this afternoon!

CYNTHIA: It's been like this for more than a month now, Ted.

TED: Five weeks! Boy, they really whiz by now.

CYNTHIA: Ted, you're sure to be fired if it keeps up much longer.

TED: Oh Cynth, not again—

CYNTHIA: But it's bound to happen—

TED: Why be an alarmist?

CYNTHIA: You can't put in ten hours a week indefinitely.

TED: What? They swallowed that heart-condition story, didn't they? Hook, line and sinker!

CYNTHIA: And they're still not suspicious?

TED: No! They're more sympathetic every day! Why, Monday they even sent the shipping clerk out to park my car for me.

CYNTHIA: They've been such nice people to work for, Ted—

TED: Don't I know it! And believe me, I feel rotten having

to lie to them, Cynth. Honestly I do. Every time I go in now and draw a week's pay, well, I get a real attack of the guilties. But—let's face it—they would never understand.

CYNTHIA: I wonder if I do, sometimes—

TED [Chucking her under the chin]: Ha, ha . . . Jesus, I nearly died, you know? I go in the other day and there behind my desk is this great big brand new Relax-o-chair! [Sings:]
> Heart of my heart,
> How I love that melody,
> Heart of my heart—

CYNTHIA: Don't, Ted! It's bad luck—

TED: OK, OK—[Runs to the window, peers out.] Where the hell is he! . . . Come on, come on. . . . Can't even see him. . . . Oh, the way those chiselers work a street, with a piece of toast here, and a fried egg there—

CYNTHIA: Ted—

TED: Yes, hon?

CYNTHIA: Say you do lose the job.

TED: We have those bonds, don't we.

CYNTHIA: They'll carry us for six months, maybe.

TED: The savings account.

CYNTHIA: Another few months.

TED: The insurance.

CYNTHIA: The insurance?

TED: And then the car.

CYNTHIA: The car?

TED: What'll we need a car for!

CYNTHIA: Oh Teddy, I'm sounding like a nag, I'm sorry—but this has got me so worried!

TED: Don't be, baby. Let me do the worrying. That job has no future, anyway. And I have some ideas, too, maybe something on my own. No one's going to starve around here, understand? I've got my health, I've got my two hands, I've got my wits about me—[Phone rings.] That damned thing again! We could do without that, too—[Answers it.] Hello. . . . Yes, speaking. . . . Encyclopedia of what? . . . Hygiene!

. . . How did my name get on *your* list, ha, ha. . . . I see.
. . . Yes, a girl . . . going on nine. . . . [*To* CYNTHIA, *covering the mouthpiece:*] Medium-soft sell. . . . [*Into the receiver:*] Uh-huh . . . uh-huh. . . . [*Rolls his eyes in mock boredom, then holds the phone at arm's length.*] He's gone into orbit. [*Resuming.*] Yeah . . . well, it's kind of you offering to drop by, Mr. Clement, but . . . Oh? . . . Is that right? . . . Uh-huh. . . . So that's included? . . . And that too, eh? . . . For how long? . . . I see. . . . And those come every month? . . . Yes . . . yes, it is. . . . Well, yes, frankly I am, Mr. Clement, now that you've—excuse me? . . . Oh, I'll give you a tentative yes on it, sure. . . . No, don't bother—just to bring over all that old promotion stuff, ha, ha, ha. . . . Just mail it to me. . . . You will? . . . Great. Then I should have it tomorrow around this time. . . . Swell. . . . Thank you, Mr. Clement—oh say, if you need to contact me again, do it by letter like a good fellow, would you? . . . Well, in case you do. . . . Thanks, Mr. Clement. . . . My pleasure. . . . Bye bye. [*Hangs up.*]

CYNTHIA: An encyclopedia.

TED: Yeah, a new one, of hygiene. It's the one volume, plus —[CYNTHIA *turns away with a sigh.*] wait, honey, listen—they send a Hygiene Monthly Report for three years, that makes thirty-six, three annual supplements, thirty-nine, the book itself, forty, plus the thing from him tomorrow, forty-one, figure a half-dozen form letters, circulars, throwaways, forty-seven— no, fifty at least! And hey, that's being conservative, Cynth!

CYNTHIA: How much is it going to cost, Ted?

TED: Seventeen dollars and fifty cents.

CYNTHIA: Would you say this book was a necessity, Ted?

TED: The book, the book, I don't care about the book—now yesterday you promised to stop that, honey . . . Christ! It's ten to nine already—[*Paces.*]

CYNTHIA: Ted—

TED: Maybe he's passed us!

CYNTHIA: He can't have, Ted—

TED: Why not! If there's nothing for me—

CYNTHIA: Ted, of course there's something. Has a day gone by—

TED: No, but I can't be sure! How can you be so sure! [*Looks out the window, paces.*]

CYNTHIA: Ted, we have to talk this out. Once and for all, Ted. We just have to now, I mean it. This whole thing is getting absolutely crazy.

TED [*Still pacing*]: Please don't nag at me, Cynthia—

CYNTHIA: When it started I tried to ignore it, Ted. Leave him alone, I said, it'll run its course, you mustn't inhibit him—

TED: I'm not answering, Cynthia—

CYNTHIA: He'll get over it, I said, like Frank with his golf or Pearl's husband with the hi-fi, or—

TED: How can you compare those measly little hobbies—

CYNTHIA: That's my whole point, Ted! I can't any more.

TED: Cynth, honey—

CYNTHIA: It's worse and worse! It's practically an obsession, Ted!

TED: But honey, what's all that wrong with it?

CYNTHIA: Look at the state you're in! Ted, when I see you like this I could cry! You're sweating, you're trembling—

TED: I never felt better in my life!

CYNTHIA: Ted, weren't you saying five minutes ago—

TED: I'm fine! I feel fine!

CYNTHIA: All right. You feel fine. But it's bleeding us dry financially, Ted. Thirty-three dollars last week for postage!

TED: Well, the more you send, Cynth—

CYNTHIA: The more they send you, I know all about it! And Ted, believe me, if it was only that, stationery and stamps, I'd say go ahead, OK, it's a luxury you need—

TED: Honey, it is!

CYNTHIA: But darling, what about the magazine subscriptions! Do you need those too? *Air Age, Publishers' Weekly,*

Glamour, True, Punch, The Beloit Poetry Journal, American Diver—

TED: Cynthia, do I smoke expensive cigars? Is my closet in there full of handmade suits?

CYNTHIA: But you don't even read them! I've seen you, Ted —you just break the wrappers and throw them away!

TED: Why do I have to read them? They're mail, that's all!

CYNTHIA: Mail, mail, mail! You're risking your job waiting at the door for it, you upset Phyllis with it just before school, you talk to me about nothing else on earth—

TED: How do you like that!

CYNTHIA: Ted, don't you see the crisis this is reaching?

TED: All this fuss over a few lousy magazines.

CYNTHIA: What about the bills from the stores, Ted? The bills you run up all over the place, for things we don't need, that you won't pay for, just to make them send you one statement after another—

TED [*Pounds the table*]:   Right! Not a penny till they threaten legal action!

CYNTHIA: There, listen to yourself! What's happened to you, Ted!

TED: I never felt better in my life! Period!

CYNTHIA: Ted, Ted . . . Oh God, how this thing has changed you.

TED: All right, it's changed me! All right! But that's what you wanted, isn't it? You weren't always after me to change now, I suppose!

CYNTHIA: Now just a minute, mister! I wanted you to get *over* certain things, to start acting your *age*, and yes, all that time you were sneaking around with Beatrice and that other one whose name you still won't tell me, I had faith that you *would* change. I was trying to help you come through that—

TED: OK! So here I am!

CYNTHIA: Congratulations.

TED: That's neither fair nor kind of you, honey—

CYNTHIA: Is this the way you used to promise me it would be? Is this my payoff for having stood by you? This ridiculous, wasteful, absolutely *childish*—

TED: Look, you know how certain words provoke me—

CYNTHIA: Who ever heard of a man of thirty-six—who's not an invalid or something, or a hermit—writing letters to pen pals all over the world? A newsy little note to every nut on the map who's willing to answer him—

TED: Listen, no fooling, do you have to call them nuts?

CYNTHIA: I never met a normal man in my life who was a pen pal!

TED: They're interesting people. You shouldn't knock them, Cynthia—

CYNTHIA: No, I ought to be thrilled you're a pen pal! P.S.— Mrs. Pen Pal says Hello and thanks!

TED: You really take the cake.

CYNTHIA: Who's the lucky one today, Ted? The captain in Nicaragua? The priest, the Indian priest? Little Nurse Hard-up in Labrador? Or that moron who—what are you shaking your head for?

TED [*Doing so sadly*]:   Wow, to be sarcastic about people making contact. Today, no less. With all those trouble spots.

CYNTHIA: They have the Peace Corps, don't they?

TED: You call that a solution?

CYNTHIA: A lot you care! As long as you get your mail every day, the world can go up in flames!

TED: Oh, now I'm another Nero. Great!

CYNTHIA: Listen to me, Ted—

TED: How come you left out the kits today, Cynth! Let's go, tick them off! The home-permanent kit, the shoe-repair kit—

CYNTHIA: Ted, I'm heartsick over this—

TED: All the do-it-yourselfies! Some not even opened yet, right? Right?

CYNTHIA: It has to stop—

TED: The Ezy-Go Shelf Kit!

CYNTHIA: Why must you do all this—

TED: The lamp-from-a-wine-bottle kit!

CYNTHIA: You're provoking me now, Ted!

TED: The—yes . . . I'm sorry.

CYNTHIA: No, you're not!

TED: I really am—

CYNTHIA: No, it's the limit—

TED: Hon, the mailman's late. I'm not feeling so hot—

CYNTHIA: Ted, if one more do-it-yourself shows up here, you'd better get a wife kit with it and start doing that yourself too! [*Turns away.*]

TED [*Lays his hand on her arm*]:   Cynthia . . . [*No response.*] Gee—ha, ha—I wish I had your sense of humor.

CYNTHIA [*Shakes his arm off*]:   No, I mean it, Ted.

TED: Ah, cut it out, Cynthia . . . [*No response.*] Besides, that's changed for the better, hasn't it?

CYNTHIA: What?

TED: You know.

CYNTHIA: Oh.

TED: Hasn't it?

CYNTHIA: I suppose.

TED: Isn't it better?

CYNTHIA: Yes.

TED: Much better.

CYNTHIA: Yes.

TED: Remember the old days!

CYNTHIA: Yes, it's better.

TED: You see?

CYNTHIA [*Turning*]:   Oh, I know, and darling, I am happy about it, but—

TED: Why can't we just count our blessings—

CYNTHIA: I try, Ted, I don't mean to nag, but sometimes it comes over me that—

TED: Kiss?

CYNTHIA [*As they embrace*]:   Oh, Ted . . .

TED [*Breaks away, dashing to the window*]:   Where's that jerk of a mailman!

CYNTHIA: He'll be along, dearest—

TED [*Peering*]:   Sneaking son of a bitch! I'll bet he's got something going for himself down the block there! Oh, it wouldn't surprise me! I've seen them in the A & P, some of those numbers—

CYNTHIA: Please be calm, darling—

TED [*Pounding the table*]:   Later and later and later! Every goddamned day! [*The top envelope falls to the floor: CYN-THIA picks it up and stares at it.*] Why can't he start at this end once in a while?

CYNTHIA: Ted—

TED [*Snatching it from her and throwing it on the table*]: Thanks—

CYNTHIA: Ted!

TED: What now!

CYNTHIA: You—you've written that letter to yourself.

TED: What? Don't be silly, there's no letter in there. Just a blank sheet of paper. [*Paces.*] Three minutes past!

CYNTHIA: Ted—whatever it is, you're sending it to yourself!

TED: Is that subversive, or something?

CYNTHIA: No, dear, but—Oh God—

TED: Please do not Oh God me any more!

CYNTHIA: I'm so confused, Ted—

TED: Look, if I send this today I'll be sure of mail tomorrow —you see? You see? You make me say it then you complain how that's all I talk about! [*Checks his watch.*] 9:05! Nine— oh—five. I swear, if he's not here in ten minutes, I'll kill him.

CYNTHIA: Ted, you mustn't!

TED: It's a figure of speech and you damn well know it! Christ! That's a *new* one . . . [*She buries her face in her hands.*] Oh, don't be upset again. Please. *Please*, Cynthia— [*Hands her his handkerchief.*] Hold on—I'll run out and see if I can spot him—

CYNTHIA: Honey, take your windbreaker—[*He runs out unheeding.* CYNTHIA *blows her nose and rushes to the phone, dials.*] Ginny, has Peter left yet? . . . Yes, please hurry. . . . Peter, thank goodness I caught you. . . . Worse and worse. . . . Peter, I can't stay on long. Can you drop in on your way? . . . OK. . . . Bless you, Peter. [*Hangs up and moves away from the phone.* TED *reenters.*]

TED: Boy, am I glad we live on a straight street! Got a glimpse of him all right—he's still down the other end. And the load on him! Whee! He's all bent over to one side, no kidding!

CYNTHIA [*Dusting*]:   That's wonderful, dear.

TED: All recovered now?

CYNTHIA: Oh, yes.

TED: Funny how things'll throw a guy sometimes. The mind blows them up out of all proportion. Here he was a little late and I was running around like a lunatic! [*Paces back and forth, humming the theme from "Moulin Rouge." Suddenly:*] We'll have to give him more than last year for Christmas.

CYNTHIA: Yes, I should say so.

TED: How much do you figure? Fifteen?

CYNTHIA: At least.

TED: OK. But I'd still rather not have him in for a drink, the way they do next door.

CYNTHIA: Whatever you say.

TED: It's too familiar. [*He paces and hums.* CYNTHIA *dusts.*] And how well can a guy do his—[*Stops in his tracks, anxious.*]

CYNTHIA: Ted—?

TED: Cynth, truth, do you ever smell it on him—?

CYNTHIA: Ted, change your mind, have some coffee.

TED: No, it makes me jumpy. [*Paces.*] All I know is, mistakes happen—

CYNTHIA: Not serious ones—

TED: Don't coddle me, please! We got Ostenelli's once. And the card for that woman I never heard of—

CYNTHIA: He took them away. He's on the ball, Ted—

TED: It's not only him! Letters get lost; it's an accepted fact! Dead letters—oh, mother, is that a way to put it! Or when they have the wrong address and they lie there for months, in a dinky hallway someplace. People won't give them a chance! Janitors! Landladies! They even throw them out half the time; sure, they don't give a damn! And then they're gone forever! You never know if—[*Phone rings; he paces.*] Let it ring, let it ring. . . . [*Paces. Suddenly answers it angrily.*] Hello! . . . Oh, good morning, Mr. Laforgue. . . . I was just about to call you. . . . No, couldn't sleep too well—that hammering in my chest kept waking me up. . . . Yes. . . . No, not this morning, I'm afraid, but— . . . Oh, George knows that file; he can handle it for me—if he doesn't mind, I mean. . . . Oh, I see. . . . Uh-huh. . . . Well, it's one of those conditions, Mr. Laforgue, they can't tell me anything so I can't be— . . . Drop in to see you Friday. . . . Aha—well, I can guess, really. . . . No. . . . No. . . . No, please don't feel badly. . . . I'm sorry too, truly I am. . . . No, no you've been very considerate . . . Gosh, that is really generous of you, sir . . . no, more than fair. . . . Oh well, why not just mail it here. . . . Yes, the less I move, the—right, thanks a million. . . . Yes I will. . . . Oh, I'll stop by when I'm up to par and say goodbye to everybody. . . . Certainly. . . . I understand, sir. . . . Goodbye. [*Slams the phone down.*] Goodbye! Goodbye! Goodbye and good—[*Grabs the wire.*] riddance to the whole—

CYNTHIA: Ted, don't—

TED [*Pulls*]:   Bunch of them! Ringing and yammering! There —[*Pulls it out of the wall.*] Goodbye!

CYNTHIA: What have you done!

TED: That's what I've done! [*Throws the phone into a corner.*] They know where to reach me and they know *how* to reach me—

CYNTHIA: Ted, God forgive me for saying this to you—

TED: Do you have to get that expression on your face? Do you have to get into that tone of voice?

CYNTHIA: Please, Ted, listen—I think you may need *help*, Ted!

TED: Help? Help? Cynthia, I need *mail!* You understand? Mail! Any kind of mail! If nothing comes through that door this morning, I'm finished! I might as well lie down and die!

CYNTHIA: You mustn't talk that way!

TED: No, I won't harm myself; no, don't worry, honey, please, I'll go away someplace, I'll send you money, you, Phyllis, I want you to have the best whatever happens, believe me—

CYNTHIA: Do you hate me, Ted—?

TED [*Clinging to her*]:   No, baby, I love you, I love you, but what can I do? I can hardly get through a Sunday now—

CYNTHIA: Don't you want to save what we have—?

TED: Yes—yes—

CYNTHIA: We have a nice home now—

TED: The day's going to come when he goes by empty-handed! It has to happen one day! And then I'm finished!

CYNTHIA: Why?

TED: Why do I breathe? Why do I sleep?

CYNTHIA: It's not the same—

TED: For me it is! Maybe it's strange, but it doesn't *feel* strange—it's just what it is—

CYNTHIA: But Ted we can beat it! I've stood by you before—

TED: Where is he! Oh, God, where is he!

CYNTHIA: You saw him, darling—

TED [*Clutching her hand*]:   Honey, what if it's today! What'll I do! Tell me! [*Going to the door.*] I'll ruin him if he isn't here soon! I'll find him and I'll kill him! [*As he reaches the door the chimes ring: he flings the door open and* PETER *enters.*]

PETER: Hiya, Teddy! Or where's the body, I should say. Hello, Cynth.

TED [*To* CYNTHIA]:   Did you have the nerve to—

PETER: Ted, hey! I was on my way to look over the new lab in Jersey, and—

TED: OK, Peter . . . it's OK. . . . I'm not sore. Come on in, sit down. [*To* CYNTHIA:] Honest, I'm not sore, sweetheart. Get Pete some coffee—

PETER: No, don't bother.

TED: Well, sit down anyway.

CYNTHIA: If you boys will excuse me, I'll clear up inside. [*Exit.* TED *laughs.*]

PETER: What?

TED: Oh, she's a sketch. I was blowing off steam and saying, you know—I'll *murder* so and so—and she really thought I was going to rub him out. [*They laugh together.*] Guess who I heard from yesterday, Pete—Charlie Adler!

PETER: Charlie Adler?

TED: Same year as us—remember him?

PETER: A sort of—?

TED: The guy with the buck teeth in Anthropology.

PETER: Oh, yeah.

TED: Getting along great, he says: two kids, owns a dry-cleaning plant—

PETER: He never hung around with us, Ted. How come you happened to hear from him?

TED: Oh, I dropped him a line. Remembrance of things past, all that, you know. I've been going through the yearbook—say, remember Jimmy Curran?

PETER: What about him, sure.

TED: Wrote him last night. I was all set to start on the D's today, but all's not so quiet on the Western Front here.

PETER: Well, you have her worried, Teddy.

TED: Ah, they all worry.

PETER: What about the job?

TED: Kaput. This morning. Had to happen, I guess.

PETER: I guess so, Ted.

TED: Had to. And frankly, I'm delighted, Pete. I was never an Organization Man—with those nosy interviews, and the questionnaires, and those, quote, social, unquote, little get-togethers they have. If *you* like it, fine: grab the security! And look, so would I, but that conformity jazz gets under my skin —you didn't see the postman when you came down the street, did you?

PETER: No, Ted, I didn't—

TED: There's a real Steppin Fetchit for you.

PETER: Now Ted—

TED: I mean it. He gets here later every day—is it like this over at your place, too?

PETER: I only have a few minutes, fellah, and—

TED: How's Ginny, Pete? I meant to ask you.

PETER: Fine, sends her love, Ted—

TED: Pete. Are you going to be an alarmist, too?

PETER: We've been pals for eighteen years, Ted—

TED: But what's the prologue for, Pete! You have some hobbies, don't you?

PETER: Ted, this isn't a hobby any more—

TED: OK! It's a way of life—you have yours, I have mine! Is there something depraved about it? Am I dirty? Do I knock my wife around?

PETER: How will you earn a living now, Ted?

TED: Start a business of my own.

PETER: What kind—mail-order?

TED: Don't think that's such a gag—here, look—[*Takes a newspaper from under the table.*] This ad must have cost a fortune, huh? Half a page? A Sunday? *The Times?* And what is the bastard selling? African violet seeds! He's making a mint—and look at this one. Here. Smaller, but he runs it every single week: Magic Auto-Cleaning Rag! These clowns are cashing in, why shouldn't I? Listen, Pete, the way I see it, automation is going to push millions of us white-collar slobs out of work, sooner or later, and once it does, well, until the economy is readjusted—maybe a matter of years—we'll be flat on our backs. So in my opinion it's a smart move now to—

PETER: What would you sell?

TED [*Pacing*]:   Don't know yet, for sure. I've been writing to a couple of guys who have products but no distribution—that would be my end. . . . I'll decide soon. But I do know this, Pete, and so do you: the whole world's liable to explode any second—

PETER: Well . . .

TED: Well, nothing! They press the wrong button? And the Chinese? The Chinese? It's liable to, Pete—tomorrow! So why not do the work we really like—while we're alive to enjoy it!

PETER [*Shaking his head*]:   One minute you talk automation, matter of years, and—

TED: Right! I'll be covered both ways! Don't you see it, Pete? You call that crazy? You think it's bohemian?

PETER: You don't look so hot, Ted . . .

TED: Jesus, don't answer me like that, Pete. You're supposed to be my friend, my very best friend!

PETER: I am, but you do look pretty shook up—

TED: Well, sure I'm shook up! What do you expect! It's fifteen minutes late—no—[*Looks at watch.*] sixteen! Sixteen! That rotten, round-shouldered, lead-footed, sadistic creeping Jesus of a mailman—

PETER: Ted, why should the mail be so important?

TED: How do I know! Everybody gets a bug in his ear sometime! That's what people are! It can be money, or women, or religion, or reading a lot, or being famous, or giving charity, or—

PETER: Getting mail.

TED: I've narrowed it down, that's all! [*Falls into a chair.*]

PETER: Level with me, Ted. How did this thing start?

TED [*In a monotone*]:   Well I used to set the alarm for 8:30 and sort of doze a little till I heard the slot click when

he pushed the mail through. And one morning a couple of
weeks ago, I was half asleep there, waiting like that, and it
all of a sudden slips into my head that if I didn't get any mail,
any at all, whatever it was, it would be—the end. Like something really horrible would happen. All in a doze this was. I
think then I reached over to Cynthia, you know, but naturally she was up already getting the kid off to school. Well, I
woke up like a shot. Had a shower, got dressed. Turned the
radio on. But the idea wouldn't go away. It was stuck in my
mind, there was nothing else I could do, and I knew it: I was
hooked. I started waiting for the mail.

PETER: Ted . . . I'm going to ask you something.

TED: Shoot, Pete. Shoot.

PETER: Ted, did it ever occur to you that there's another
word "male" . . . ?

TED: Mail . . . [*Leaping to his feet.*] MALE! By God,
Pete, that's right! Male! Male! [*Laughs with embarrassment and pleasure.*] Can you beat that! How could I be so
dumb!

PETER: Oh, you weren't so dumb half-asleep that morning—

TED: Imagine! Imagine!

PETER: *You* made the connection—

TED: I must have! Sure!

PETER: And you went on this postal kick—

TED: Pete, it's fantastic—

PETER: And it changed your whole life!

TED: Boy, the human mind!

PETER: *You* thought you had to get yourself *mail*—

TED: Oh, I knew it was that the second you said it—

PETER: Maybe a little sort of insecure, eh, old pal?

TED: About m-a-l-e.

PETER: Yes?

TED: Well . . .

PETER: Don't want to step on your toes now, Ted—

TED: No, no, go ahead—

PETER: That affair with Beatrice—?
TED: Uh huh—Uh huh—
PETER: And the other one last year—
TED: Yes—I get it—
PETER: Proving something.
TED: Male.
PETER: That's it.
TED: And—and you think all the wild stuff at college—?
PETER: Could be, Ted—
TED: Holy mackerel—
PETER: Even then!
TED: Pete, that's some head you've got on your shoulders—
PETER: Well, when you're outside a thing—
TED: No, no—
PETER: And what the hell, it's a common pattern—
TED: No kidding—?
PETER: Sure—a screwed-up homelife like you had?
TED: Remember?
PETER: The way your old man was?
TED: I'm with you, I'm with you—
PETER: Some example for a boy—
TED: And what about her!
PETER: That well of affection!
TED: She left her mark, all right!
PETER: Try and trust a woman after—
TED: Oh, Pete, couldn't do it—
PETER: Just grabbed for what you missed—
TED: All over, yeah—
PETER: Made them love you, then you hurt them—
TED: Every goddamned one!
PETER: Made them hurt you back—
TED: Right back! Right back!
PETER: Made yourself miserable!
TED: Miserable, right! Right, right—[*Paces.*] absolutely—
my God!—so I've just been—wait—no, first I—no—no, *first*

it—no, oh Pete, Pete, it's so disconnected—you better get it down! On paper!

PETER: What?

TED: On paper! For me, Pete! OK? The whole story! I'll see it much clearer when I see it written down—

PETER: But Ted—

TED: Not now, you have to leave, I know, but tonight, tonight, do it after dinner, Pete! Send me a letter with all the details!

PETER: Ted, be serious—

TED: I'm asking you a favor—

PETER: But that's not the point—

TED: Peter, I'm a drowning man! Help me!

PETER: Ted, you *do* need help—

TED: I do and then I get some, but then I need some more—help me, Pete, help me—

PETER: Ted, I'm not a doctor!

TED: Won't you send me the letter?

PETER: You need a trained doctor!

TED: Then send me a doctor's name! Send me anything— [*Flies to the window.*]

PETER: Ted—

TED: There he is! A few doors down—

PETER: Ted, I'd better be—

TED: Oh, sure, Pete, fine—[*Shakes his hand warmly as he leads him to the door.*] And thank you, Pete. Sincerely. Where'd you say you were going?

PETER: Jersey.

TED [*Opens the door*]:   Drop me a card when you get there, OK?

PETER: I'll call in later, Ted. [*Going.*] So long—

TED [*Calling after him*]:   Eighteen years! Remember that, Pete! [*Closes the door.* CYNTHIA *reenters, carrying a duster and an extension cord, which she plugs into the wall.*]

CYNTHIA: How did it go?

TED: Ah, the guy's a real prince, no getting around it. Had a swell talk. And you-know-who is only three doors down now.

CYNTHIA: What did he say?

TED: Pete? Oh, agreed about the job—gave a few tips on some plans I have—

CYNTHIA: And about the—the other?

TED: Ha! We had a good laugh about that—it's more a way of life than a hobby, he says—[*Chuckles as he goes to window, stops short.*] Ah! Going up to Hoffman's there now—What a morning, hey, honey?

CYNTHIA: Yes. Didn't talking with Pete—help you any?

TED [*Peering out*]: Can't tell you how much! Cleared up a lot—What's keeping him at Hoffman's, the rascal!

CYNTHIA: Oh, I do hope he'll have something.

TED: Don't worry! Don't worry, got that feeling in my bones, the old—there! Now, swing around to Spencer—[*Half-turns.*] You OK, sweetie? No more spats? Kiss? [*She comes to him and kisses his cheek as he goes on looking out.*] Quick! Take a look before he—did you see him?

CYNTHIA: Yes.

TED: That's what I call a good face! You know? I mean, it's a *face*. One look, you can tell you've got a really decent Joe there—I think he'll have something, huh?

CYNTHIA: He should, Ted, yes—

TED: All those names I called him, a guy like that—

CYNTHIA: Ted, you don't even know his name—

TED: So what, I can—whoops!—yeah, through with Spencer! Come on, Cynth—[*Seizes her.*] a fast tango, the band is terrific here—Da-da-da-DUM-da-dee, da-da-da-DUM-da-daaa—[*They dance.*] Hey, watch that knee, Jack—

CYNTHIA [*Laughs*]: Oh, you are a case—[*Breaking away.*] Come on, I have things to do—

TED: OK, OK—

CYNTHIA: Everything will be all right, won't it, Ted?

TED: Can't miss!

CYNTHIA: I love you so, Ted, but—

TED: But nothing! And—[*Smacks her rump.*] what do you know about love, you big Polack! [*Returns to the window.*] Go ahead and clean, honey—he's back on the sidewalk now—heading for next-door—no, he's saying Hello to some kid—Say Goodbye, say goodbye—Ah, there he goes!—Gee, what a packet for them—Well—We're next—[CYNTHIA *watches from a doorway at one side as* TED *remains fixed at the window.*] —Imagine how it's going to pour in around Christmas—wow —Extra men put on—four, five, six deliveries a day sometimes—toward the end—they really do it in style, huh?—And it's legitimate stuff, too—all those cards—cards, cards, cards, just flowing right in. Boy, you could sit behind the door all day here, catching them, one after another—and you don't have to con people for them—or beg—or cook up anything . . . [*Breaks off, peering.*]

CYNTHIA: He'll be through there in a minute—

TED: All different shapes, sizes—beautiful designs on a lot of them, too—I just love them—and the messages, the way you get the whole range from Best Holiday Wishes to Gentle Jesus Meek and Mild, keep your fingers crossed honey—

CYNTHIA: Yes.

TED: Yes—one after the other—through the P.O. and then to you—and then, reading the names of who sent them, one by one, no matter who it is, even the business ones, the people sort of change for a minute, in your mind, the way they would if you saw them all riding past you on a merry-go-round—it's sort of corny but you—hold it! He's finished there! He's coming! Oh Jesus—wait—why doesn't he—ah!—Honey he's reaching in—I think we're all right!—wait—Yes! We're all right! —ha—Go on with your work—Here he comes!—Go *on*, honey —[*Shoos her out without turning.*] I'll have a little fun with him today—[*Exit* CYNTHIA. TED *ducks under the window, crouches before the door, waits a moment, then swiftly thrusts his left arm up to the elbow through the slot. Calling through it:*] Surprise! [*Instantly the roar of a vacuum-cleaner starts up offstage.* TED *tries to extricate his arm but cannot. His cries can barely be heard over the roar.*] No, no! Don't hand it to me! I'm stuck. STUCK! Wait! [*He reaches across with his free right hand and gives a ferocious yank to the doorknob: it comes off in his grasp. He tries to fit it back on, fumbles and fails, then throws it down.*] I can't . . . CYNTHIA! She can't hear me! Come around! AROUND! [*He gestures as best he can through the slot: the* MAILMAN *appears at the window and* TED *makes a gesture for him to open it and enter.*] YES! IT'S ALL RIGHT! [*The* MAILMAN *opens the window and steps in. Laying down his bag and* TED's *pile of mail he quickly helps* TED *free his arm from the slot.* TED *ruefully rubs his elbow and thanks him; the* MAILMAN *replies with a gesture of "I can't hear a thing." All smiles,* TED *answers with a "She's at it with that vacuum" gesture; the* MAILMAN *nods and smiles with understanding.* TED *pulls out his wallet as if to offer him a tip, but the* MAILMAN *declines with a bit of friendly embarrassment, then hands* TED *his mail with a gesture of "Plenty today."* TED *beams with pleasure, then jokingly embraces the* MAILMAN *like a French general. They laugh heartily, soundlessly.* TED *carefully helps the* MAILMAN *on with his bag, points out the broken doorknob with a shrug, and gallantly assists him back over the windowsill. They shake hands. The* MAILMAN *goes.* TED *waves to him, closes the window, then drifts toward the wallsocket as he examines his mail. He kneels beside it, still going through the cards, letters and magazines with steadily increasing happiness; then, without diverting his gaze from these, he reaches out and pulls the extension-cord plug from its socket. The roar from within dies immediately and* CYNTHIA *reenters. She wears a smart black dress, her face is fully made-up, and she unbinds, as she walks toward him in silence, the kerchief from her head.* TED, *still at his task, does not look up. By the time she has kneeled beside him he has begun to hum, softly under his breath, the themesong from* Moulin Rouge, *and her long hair has already cascaded down to her shoulders.*]

CURTAIN

Match Play
Lee Kalcheim

CAST:

Marty .... Tony Musante
Jill .... Rosemary Forsyth
Dad .... Avery Schreiber

Directed by Edward Parone

First presented at Theater 1964 Playwrights Unit Workshop,
May 17, 1964.

People in the Play:

DAD (Mr. Gillman)
MARTY, his son
JILL WICKERSHAM

Living room of a very comfortable home in Riverdale. Book-cases, hi-fi, couches, chairs of mixed contemporary and antique. Kitchen, hallway, upstairs are off.

MR. GILLMAN *is poised with a golf club in his hand, putting toward one of several indoor golf holes.*

He continues putting as we hear the door slam and a voice singing offstage.

MARTY: Good King Wenceslas las las las . . . las las las las laaass las. [MARTY *enters with* JILL, *stopping at the doorway.*] Mind if we play through??

DAD: Eh? You back already?

MARTY: Already? It's three o'clock. I brought you a caddy. [*Escorts* JILL.] This is Miss Jill Wickers. . . .

JILL: Wickersham.

MARTY: Wickersham. This is my father, Ben Hogan.

DAD: How do you do.

JILL: This house is magnificent. Look at that fireplace. Does it work? [*Bending to look under it.*] I could put my whole apartment in here.

MARTY: That might be fun. We could sit here and watch it burn.

MARTY: Can I get you a drink? ⎱ [*Together.*]
DAD: Would you like a drink? ⎰

JILL: Ahhh—I don't know.

MARTY: I'll get it, Dad. . . . [*Going to bar.*] Scotch and what?

JILL: Yes. I'll have that.

MARTY: Little bit of Scotch and what for the lady. Go easy on the what.

DAD: You look a little wet. Raining hard?

149

JILL: Marty had the top down—I'm not getting the rug wet or anything?

DAD: It's all right.

JILL: You have a Christmas tree somewhere? It's probably a giant.

DAD: Well, I'm Jewish.

JILL: Oh—sorry.

DAD: It's all right.

MARTY [*Handing her drink*]:   What are you?

JILL: I'm Methodist.

MARTY: So am I. . . . Hey! You're not supposed to drink.

JILL: I'm a drinking Methodist.

MARTY: Jillsie here is from Ohio—now of Manhattan and the Radio City Music Hall.

JILL: I'm a Rockette. I don't look it, do I?

MARTY: He wouldn't know. He's never seen one.

JILL: You've never been to the Music Hall?

DAD: I don't go to the movies.

MARTY: We have our own projector. See, that's all film up there on the top shelf.

JILL: Well, you'll have to come sometime. You never saw the Christmas show?

MARTY: He's verrry cagey.

JILL: It's quite a spectacle. Marty saw it. In the final number I play a sheep. I kind of dance out, and the lights come up and the manger shows through the scrim and then the scrim goes up and I dance over to the manger with the other sheep and I sit right next to the Virgin Mary, she's one of my friends, Barbara. We draw lots to see who'll play that part. Barbara won. She gets an extra five dollars for playing the Virgin Mary. And then the singers sing "Silent Night"—and it's very pretty. Really. We do the usual line at the end. It's the same for every show. Just different costumes. We're all dressed like sequinned Santa Clauses. For Christmas. I go to school, too. I love your home.

DAD: Why, thank you.

JILL [*Looks up and around*]:   Lovely . . .

DAD: Why don't you show her around, Marty?

MARTY: Huh? Ah . . . Sure. How about the grand tour?
We usually leave that up to my mother. She's got a whole
spiel, but—We've heard it so many times. Ready—one, two,
three.

MARTY and DAD: —"This is the third oldest house in the
community, built after the original mansion and the carriage
house for the son and daughter-in-law of Mr. and Mrs. Win-
throp-Harmon."

MARTY: Aren't we good listeners?

JILL: Can I see the rest?—I'd also like to. Do you have a—
john?

MARTY: Do we? We have five. You can take your pick.
C'mon. [*Takes her hand and starts out.* DAD *picks up club;*
MARTY *stops.*] Hey—Did you play this afternoon?

DAD: Uh huh.

MARTY [*To* JILL]:   Thirty degrees. He plays golf.

DAD: I was trying out that new thermo underwear. Terrific
stuff.

JILL: You play all winter?

DAD: Sure. Thermo underwear. We play in the snow. They
have red balls so you can play in the snow.

JILL: That's silly.

MARTY: Don't tell *him* that. He would play during a blitz.
C'mon. [*They start out.* MARTY *fires a glance back and smiles
at his father before he is yanked off.* DAD *starts putting again.
Offstage:*] This is the stairway. You know, I used to slide down
this banister. Very good for that.

JILL [*Offstage*]:   Is that stained glass?

MARTY [*Offstage*]:   Oh . . . Yeah. We're very religious—
That's the den down there. And—this is the dining room.

JILL [*Offstage*]:   Ooooh. Look at that chandelier.

[DAD *stops putting, remembers something, and goes over to*

one corner to a carton; brings it back and puts it on table.]

MARTY [*Offstage*]:   Somebody important ate on this table once. I don't remember—Lafayette or somebody. D'you like the wall paper?

JILL [*Offstage*]:   It's beautiful.

MARTY [*Offstage*]:   I hate it. . . . On to the kitchen. I must warn you. It looks just like a kitchen. Only it's big.

[DAD *opens carton and pulls out a huge egg warmer which looks like a large copper or silver egg. It opens in the middle and has a heating device underneath it. The kids' voices in the kitchen are unintelligible, but we hear them laugh as they start coming back.*]

MARTY [*Offstage*]:   It's true. There are mice in our kitchen. They come up here from the Bronx on vacation—over there. [*Reentering by himself.*] Tour over. Ehhhh. What the hell is that?

DAD: That, my friend, is your mother's latest Second Avenue treasure. It was delivered today.

MARTY: She buys a lot of stuff, but you usually know what it is, even if we don't need it.

DAD: I wish I had a share of A T & T for every coffee mill in this house.

MARTY: Are you insinuating that there might be something *wrong* with a Tiffany lamp in the john?

DAD: What is it, Marty? Take a guess.

MARTY: Well, it's an old something—right?

DAD [*Laughs*]:   You'll never guess in a million years.

MARTY: Give me a hint.

DAD [*Laughs*]:   No—no. You guess.

MARTY: I don't know—what it is. A do it yourself globe. Come on, what is it?

DAD: That—is an egg warmer!

MARTY: An egg warmer? For what, an ostrich egg?

DAD: Look [*Opens the top half.*] See—all those little slots for eggs.

MARTY: I have two questions. First of all: Who the hell's
going to eat all those eggs? And why do you want to keep
them warm?

DAD: Boiled eggs, I guess—keep them warm.

MARTY: We don't eat boiled eggs. You don't think Mother's
actually going to use it for that. Some hen would have a
hernia keeping this thing filled.

DAD: Probably put a plant in it—or a lamp or something. I
don't know.

MARTY: Make a nice stud box eh? An egg warmer—Ahhh
. . . You going up?

DAD: Well . . . Yes, I guess I'd better get to bed. . . .
Don't make too much noise down here—huh?

MARTY: Oh, we'll be verrry quiet.

DAD: I mean if you're going to play music. Not too loud—

MARTY: You get your sleep sport. No excuses when we get
out on the course.

DAD: Say goodnight to Jill for me—and—[*Egg warmer.*]
keep an eye on that thing. 'Night. [*Salutes.* DAD *exits.* MARTY
goes to warmer. Examines it. Looks inside, sticks head in.]

MARTY: Hello in there—Helloooooooo. Merry Christmas.
[*Slaps it shut.*] Good King Wenceslas looked out—over everybody. Over over over over over everybody. . . . Deck the halls
with boughs of holly Fa la la la la—and tie one on. [JILL
enters.] There she is—all combed and pretty. Did you tittle?
My old man said goodnight. He holed out.

JILL: He's very nice. Is he coming back?

MARTY: He went to bed.

JILL: Oh. . . . [*Looking around.*] Did somebody read all
these books?

MARTY: That is a false wall. You press a button behind *Tale
of Two Cities* and Jerry Colonna comes out with the cavalry.
Did you see *Road to Rio?*

JILL: What's that?

MARTY: It's a movie. Bob Hope, Dorothy Lamour. You
want to see it? I'll pull out the projector. The film's up there.

In this picture, Jerry Colonna rides to the rescue of Bing Crosby. He rides and rides and rides—and just at the end of the picture, he gets there too late. That breaks me up. Want to see it?

JILL: No. [*Examining books.*] Look at this book. It's signed by F. Scott Fitzgerald.

MARTY: Yeah?

JILL: If I had this book, I'd sleep with it.

MARTY: What's that, another Methodist's trick? C'mere.

JILL: What?

MARTY: Come here. Stop looking at the books.

JILL: Did you read this? *Green Mansions?*

MARTY: Yeah, yeah. C'mere.

JILL: You didn't read it.

MARTY: I read it. It's about the jungle and this weird girl who swings from trees—a lovely book. I read it.

JILL: Who was the boy in the book?

MARTY: I don't know. Tony Perkins.

JILL [*To movies*]:   You have that up there, too.

MARTY: Come on . . . come over and sit.

JILL: I want to look around a little. All right?

MARTY: Look—ah—Is this what you came out here for? Just to look around?

JILL: You invited me.

MARTY: I invited you because—You want to know why?

JILL: Why?

MARTY: Because you have great legs. By my standards, great legs. I have a thing for dancers. [*Going to her.*]

JILL: Well, hold onto your thing and keep calm. Let me look around.

MARTY: Look honey, I'm not going to bite you. Keep the Christmas spirit. You know, it's nobler to give than to receive.

JILL: That conflicts with my New Year's resolution.

MARTY: I can't figure you out. You're very—aloof. When I put your coat on in the club, you kissed like a trooper. I thought it was gonna happen in the cloakroom. I should have kept you in town. That ride cooled you off.

JILL: That's right. . . . Where's this go. [*Peeking in hall.*]

MARTY: To the stairs.

JILL: Who lives up there?

MARTY: Well, my father, my mother, when she's here . . . our maid . . . and our decrepit old cocker spaniel. One hundred and twelve years old. A real tiger.

JILL: What's this?

MARTY: Hi-fi. Put something on.

JILL: It won't wake anybody?

MARTY: It's all right. My old man's used to it. I got him so he thinks he's *supposed* to hear Ray Charles at three in the morning. Push.

JILL: Here?

MARTY: Just push everything. If the record doesn't play, something will happen. [*He goes to her to dance.*]

JILL: There goes—Ooop—what is it?

MARTY: Probably Ray Charles. Let's dance.

JILL: All right. Careful.

MARTY: Like a porcupine—verrry carefully . . .

[*Record drops, plays. It is a Brandenburg.*]

MARTY: What is this??

JILL: It's not Ray Charles.

MARTY: Not *my* Ray Charles. . . . Ahhh . . . screw it. . . . Let's dance. [*He begins dancing.*]

JILL: Hey, you can't dance to this.

MARTY: Why not?

JILL: That's—that's Bach.

MARTY: You think he'd object??

JILL: You can't *dance* to this.

MARTY: I think we're doing very well.

JILL: Marty.

MARTY: Go ahead—kick.

JILL: Come on.

MARTY: Go ahead. Kick. [*She does.*] Yeah! [*He claps.*] Over my head. Kick over my head. [*She does. He ducks a little.*] Yeah!!!

JILL: You don't have to duck.

MARTY: Did I duck? Did I duck?? Do it again.

JILL: That's enough.

MARTY: Come on. [*He takes her and dances furiously to Bach. Backs her up to the couch.*]

JILL: Marty . . .

[*He holds up his hands, she goes out from his pursuit, but he grabs her hand.*]

MARTY: Don't go away.

JILL: You're such a smart ass . . .

MARTY: I'm dancing.

JILL [*Turns it off*]:   Is this your record?

MARTY: My old lady's.

JILL: I'd like to meet her.

MARTY: I doubt it. She's in Miami now—schmoosing—Heh! I can't figure you out. One minute you've got *me* cornered in a cloakroom—and the next you're acting like a goddam nun—ehh—Hey—isn't that a good name for a woman that doesn't get any. Nun. [*Laughs.*] Get it—nunnnn. [*Laughs.*] Come on, baby. Loosen up. [*JILL is getting another drink.*] Thata girl. Heyyyyy, I got an idea—How about some golf? Really. Anyone can learn—Here hold this. [*Gives her his drink, goes and gets father's club and balls he left in the corner, gathers portable holes, back to JILL.*] Just let me—ah —we'll throw the old hole down here. We call this "instant pebble beach." My father and I play for money. He already owes me two thousand dollars. I'll put another hole back here behind the couch. It's a drop hole. You stand on the couch and shoot. OK. Now. Club—Ball—Drink—All set??

JILL: This is ridiculous.

MARTY: Come on—we'll play for stakes.

JILL: You mean money?

MARTY: Money—or ah—we can just try match play. You
know—whoever wins gets—ah—whoever wins gets whoever
loses—

JILL: I don't play golf.

MARTY: Come on. Come on. You need a caddy? I'll wake
the maid. She'll come down and carry your clubs around.

JILL: Go ahead, you play. I'll look around.

MARTY: Come on. We'll play strip golf. You ever play strip
golf?

JILL: What's that?

MARTY: Like strip poker. You lose a hole, you take something off. If you've never played, it's great. You oughta be
naked by the twelfth hole. Come on—I'll give you a handicap.

JILL: I already have a handicap. And I wish he'd calm
down. . . .

MARTY: Very wit-ty. . . . Hey, baby, you're miles from nowhere. You can look at books in the public library. [*Goes to
her with club.*] Here, you'll probably beat the pants off me.
That's good! Beat the pants. . . . Forget it. . . . Come on
cookie. You start here.

JILL: Do you play golf with every girl you meet?

MARTY: Not if I can avoid it. Come on now—I hear Methodists are great golfers. Arnold Palmer. Jack Nicklaus. Sam
Snead—all Methodists, right? . . . You go first.

JILL: Where?

MARTY: Shoot toward the first hole. Over there in front of
the couch. [JILL *sets herself, lines up, swings—and misses.*]
You're supposed to keep your eye on the ball.

JILL: Oh—OK, OK—OK. . . . [*This time she swings very
easily, keeping eye on the ball, in fact just pushing the ball
right to the cup.*] Hey, this is great! !

MARTY: See? . . . [MARTY *gets up on couch.*]

JILL: Where's the next hole?

MARTY: Drop hole. I'll show you. [MARTY *stands on couch*

*and puts ball on back of couch, aiming toward hole in back
of it on the floor.*] Now this is very difficult because you have
to choke up on the club to hit it. . . . You just knock the ball
off the back—and into the cup—if you want a hole in one—
which is absolutely necessary—since par for this hole is one.

JILL: Does this keep you up nights? Designing these shots?

MARTY: My old man and I used to have three-day tourna-
ments. No sleep. We had these holes spread out all over the
house. We had water hazards—we filled the bathtub and put
the hole in the soap dish. You had to chip the shot or it fell in
the tub. Oh, and in the kitchen—what a hole. The garbage
disposal. That was a long shot. You stand at the doorway from
the dining room and you've got a good twenty-foot shot to
the sink—and a forty-dollar plumber's bill if you sink it.

JILL: I don't believe any of that.

MARTY: I shit you not. Three days we played. My mother
was in Miami playing cards. We gave the maid three days off.
She practically cried—she cried more than the day FDR died.
And I won. And on a drop shot. I mean a real drop shot.
From the third floor landing—down the stairwell. Try that
into one of these holes. The ball bounces out every single
time. Know how I won?

JILL: I can't imagine.

MARTY: I cheated. I put chewing gum on the ball. Plunk—
stuck like a trooper. You know what I won on that game? That
car. He went out and got that car. We were so sleepy we
practically cracked it up coming home. What a time. . . .
Ah—watch [*Shoots.*] See—it pops out. But I can't cheat.
You're in on the secret. We'll try for a bogey. Tap mine in.
[JILL *takes a club.* MARTY *observes. Standing in back of couch,
she prepares to hit it.*] Easy . . .

JILL: Marty—what does your father do?

MARTY: What do you want to know that for?

JILL: I don't know.

MARTY: If it'll make you shoot any better. He makes boxes.

Paper boxes. Lots and lots of boxes. And if you've ever stopped to think how many boxes we use every day, you'd get a pretty good idea of the kind of thing my old man has going for him.

JILL: In my A & P there is a mountain of them.

MARTY: That's my old man's mountain, cookie.

JILL: Is it magic?

MARTY: What?

JILL: Nothing . . . you wouldn't understand.

MARTY: What wouldn't I understand? I understand everything. What? What?

JILL: Nothing. I was being . . . Magic—you know *The Magic Mountain*. You see, you don't understand.

MARTY: That's Horace Mann—right? Horace Mann wrote that about a tubercular asylum—right? So what don't I understand?

JILL: Nothing.

MARTY: Did you read it?

JILL: I'm reading it now. It's by Thomas Mann.

MARTY: What'd I say? What's the difference? It's a good book. Look, honey, I'm not a gangster, you know. I went to three different colleges. Something rubbed off. I may have never graduated but I went. As a matter of fact, I read that damn book twice. Once for a German literature course and once for a philosophy course. I used the same paper in each college. I'm sure that's the book. About a—rest home, right?

JILL: Yes.

MARTY: Shoot, baby. . . .

JILL [*Shoots, and shot hits wall*]:   Whoops!

MARTY: Spraying shots like a demon, she stormed about the course. . . . I'll get it. You—Where is it? I thought it went into the shelf.

JILL: Let me look. [*They go to shelf and look.*] Oooh, whose guitar is this?

MARTY: Ummm. Nobody's. My mother got it for decoration.

JILL [*Picks it up and strums it*]:   It's out of tune.

MARTY: Doesn't have to be in tune to look good. [JILL *begins tuning the guitar.*] Some help you are.

JILL: I quit, anyhow. I won the first hole.

MARTY: We lost a ball—that's a penalty. One stroke . . . ehhh . . . I'll get another. [*He goes to closet to get ball.* JILL *tunes guitar and starts singing.*]

JILL:

> Go to sleepy, little ba-by
> Go to sleepy, little ba-by
> When you wake
> We'll patty patty cake
> And ride a shiny little po-o-ny.

MARTY: Hey . . . that's nice. [*Turning from closet.*] Come here. I got a song. Maybe you know it.

JILL: I don't know a lot of songs.

MARTY: Come here. [*He goes to her.*] You play this? Listen . . .

> I stuck my finger
> In a woodpecker's hole.
> The woodpecker said
> "Goddam your soul.
> Take it out,
> Take it out,
> Reeemove it . . . !"

You don't know that. That's a great song.

JILL: I can imagine.

MARTY: You got to hear the rest of it.

JILL: I'm sure you do.

MARTY: What were you playing. . . . Go ahead. . . . You don't know any Christmas carols?

JILL: Not on the guitar.

MARTY: Go ahead—sing what you were singing. . . .

JILL:

> *Go to sleepy, little baby*
> *Go to sleepy, little baby*

MARTY: Wait a minute—wait—can't you move it a little—
you know . . . [*Faster.*]

> *Go to sleepy, little—baby*
> *Go to sleepy, little—ba-a-by*

JILL: Marty, it's a lullaby.
MARTY: Pardon me. OK. Go ahead.
JILL and MARTY:

> *Go to sleepy, little baby*
> *Go to sleepy, little baby*

JILL:

> *When you wake we'll*
> *Paddy paddy cake*
> *And . . .* [*Says to him:*]
> *Ride a shiny little pony.*

MARTY [*Sings*]:   Ride—a shiny little pony . . .
JILL: That's very nice. . . .
MARTY: Yeah?
JILL: Try another.
MARTY: You play—I'll get the—extra balls. Where'd you
learn to play that thing?
JILL: Between shows. I learned in the dressing room. . . .
MARTY: That's where you read Thomas Mann too, huh?
JILL: Uh huh.
MARTY: I'd like to see your dressing room—It must look like
the national cultural center. You ought to do a stand up.
Sing, play, read, dance—all at once. And maybe with practice
you wind up with a hole in one. Here, here's another ball.
JILL: I don't want to play any more.

MARTY: You want that thing, take it home. My mother'd love to find another one.

JILL: I have one, thank you.

MARTY: Is that a good one?

JILL: I don't know. I just started playing.

MARTY: It's probably a good one. Take it home. My present.

JILL: I'm used to mine—thank you . . .

MARTY: Look, if you're going to play, play something lively —That song is very morose, you know. What do you know? Come on, let's sit on the couch and sing. Come on.

JILL: That's all right. I don't want to play any more.

MARTY: Come on. [*Taking her hand and pulling her to come to couch.*] We'll sing it up on the couch.

JILL: I don't want to play any more.

MARTY: All right, so don't play the guitar. Let's play without it!

JILL: Marty!

MARTY [*Tries to embrace her and she struggles; imitating her*]: "Marty"—Come on, what are you keeping it for?

JILL [*Breaking away*]:   What's the matter with you? You're not an animal.

MARTY: Well, you make me an animal. I ask you like a polite human being and all you do is run away. So you make me an animal.

JILL: Well, I don't like that. . . .

MARTY: What's the matter with you? You don't want to do anything. You don't want to dance. You don't want to play golf. You don't want to sing. . . . What do you want to do?

JILL: I would love to dance with you—or golf—or sing—but you don't want to enjoy any of those things. They're just an excuse for you to get your hands somewhere.

MARTY: What the hell, am I supposed to run after you for a year until I get to grab something?

JILL: Marty, I never met you before tonight, remember?

MARTY: I had good references. You didn't have to go out

with me. What did your friend Sheila say about me? Did she
say I'm an animal? I'm sure she didn't. She said, "He's loaded
and he'll probably take you all over town and show you a
good time . . . and if he likes you, he'll drive you up to his
home in Riverdale." I did every one of those things. Right?
No surprise to you. Right? And all the while, you drink a few,
you talk a little, you come on like a swinging little girl. I get
you in the cloakroom at the club and you come on like gang
busters. I bring you out here—and if I don't watch out you're
gonna be sitting in a corner doing needlepoint. Right?

JILL: I had a lot to drink, Marty.

MARTY: So drink some more. You bore me sober.

JILL: I'm sorry.

MARTY: Ahhh, look. I'm not a sex maniac—I want to have
some fun. You're a good-looking girl—We had a good time.
Now, why stop?

JILL: Marty . . . I don't think you understand me.

MARTY: Jill, I don't think you've been listening. For the past
five minutes I've been *saying* I don't understand you.

JILL: I mean—you don't understand—really.

MARTY: I don't want to understand you. I just want to play
with you.

JILL: Not like this.

MARTY [*Mimicking*]:   "Not like this!" Like what? Like the
Bells of St. Mary's. You mean to tell me that every one of
your friends at the Radio City Music Hall who comes out
every night in a little bit of sequins and kicks up her heels—is,
deep down inside—an inhibited little girl who just wants someone to understand her?

JILL: Of course not.

MARTY: How the hell do you have the guts to be a Rockette?
Besides the fact that it is the worst show I've ever seen—
whether you like it or not—you are a sexual image.

JILL: I'm nothing but a dancer. . . .

MARTY: You think they pack the Music Hall just to see you move gracefully? Did you ever see the crowd on a matinee day? It's not all screaming school kids and fat mothers. Ever look in the third balcony—filled with dirty old men—all smoking pot—letching at you. . . .

JILL: Very funny. . . .

MARTY: You think I'm kidding. You ask someone from Iowa what a Rockette is—they'd say—"Oh yeah, those girls with the legs."

JILL: The Rockettes are known for their precision.

MARTY: Let's have some, huh?

JILL: There are some very talented dancers in that troupe— who expect to dance in concert. We're not exotic dancers, you know.

MARTY: Ohhh, you are right! You are not exotic. I'd say that's about the squarest routine I've ever seen—but you still have an image—of legs—of bodies.

JILL: And that's why you took me out—because I'm a Rock-ette—a body.

MARTY: Come on, give me some credit. Sheila said, "She's a Rockette," like she was apologizing. She told me you were a smart girl. You were going to school, right—Hunter or some-thing, right? You've educated yourself—that's noble. You're a clean-cut American girl. That's very noble. You've got nice legs. That's *really* noble.

JILL: Marty . . . take me home.

MARTY: Come on—get serious, will you?

JILL: Marty. I want you to take me home.

MARTY [*Goes into his wallet*]: Here—here's twenty bucks. Buy yourself a cab.

JILL: I don't want that. I want you to take me home.

MARTY: Take it. [*He stuffs it in her dress and she pulls back.*]

JILL: Marty, stop that.

MARTY: I want you to take it! You'll need it. [*He goes to get drink.*]

JILL: Marty, please take me home.

MARTY: Look—I'm sorry if I insulted you in any way—but I'm not leaving here tonight. Not yet. So if you want to go home now. . . . You go out in the street and wave that twenty-dollar bill. Some one is bound to stop. If that doesn't work, stick out your leg, like a production number. Someone may recognize it.

JILL: Please, Marty.

MARTY [*Turns with drink*]: Look—why don't you have a little drink—we'll sit and chat. I'll speak very softly—I'll sit on my hands—We'll discuss all these books. I'll read from the Bible—what? Come on—take this. [*Offers drink; she turns away and begins to cry.*] Oh, for Christ sake. . . . Look, I said I'm sorry. [*She continues crying.*] Will you please stop crying. I'm sorry. [*Continues.*] Look, will you stop that, for Christ. I said I'm sorry and I don't even know what I'm sorry for. Now the least you could do is stop and tell me what you're crying for! [*Continues.*] Please stop . . . please . . . pretty please . . . with sugar . . . with Scotch . . . huh? [*She stops, whimpers a little, stops.*]

JILL: I'm sorry.

MARTY: I said it first—but you go ahead. . . . [JILL *just walks over, takes drink out of his hand, goes to couch and sits.*] I'll be goddamned. What is with you, woman?

JILL [*Sipping a drink*]: Marty . . . I want to get married.

MARTY: Oh. Would you like me to call a few witnesses?

JILL: I want to get married. I don't care about seeing every nightclub in New York. I don't care about indoor golf. I don't particularly like to drink—and I don't like to wrestle. . . . Why couldn't you just be—oh—forget it. I do sound like the virgin queen.

MARTY: What—what did Sheila tell you about me?

JILL: Just what you said she did.

MARTY: So—what are you doing here? You knew this is where you'd end up.

JILL: Marty, don't be silly. I'm not going to marry a corpse.

I want him to be living and breathing—maybe even—drinking a little—and—you—have—good things about you.

MARTY: I have good things about me? How nice. I think Miss Herbott said that to me in the fourth grade: "Martin, you have good things about you." . . . Then she washed my mouth out with soap. I called her an old bat.

JILL: That's what I'm going to be—an old bat. Every man in this town just wants to grab on to something.

MARTY: And the girls don't?

JILL: I'd like to find a sensible husband.

MARTY: You wouldn't like to grab some money on the way down the aisle?

JILL: I certainly would. I wouldn't have gone out with you if you weren't well off—or at least—at a good job. Listen, you don't know how many actors have asked me out.

MARTY: They're all queer!

JILL: Not all. But most of them are poor. And they'll stay that way. Who needs that? I'd like to have kids. I'd like a considerate man—with a head on his shoulders—with a respectable job.

MARTY: Why don't you cruise up and down Wall Street and solicit? You know, take bids.

JILL: I went out with a broker. He bored me to death. Three advertising men, two accountants, a lawyer, six or seven doctors, all discussing their favorite patients. I get bored very easily.

MARTY: I didn't bore you, right?

JILL: No, you didn't bore me.

MARTY: So, I'm the perfect husband, right?

JILL: I couldn't marry you in a million years.

MARTY: Thanks—I wouldn't wait. In a million years I'd be way past menopause.

JILL: Ohhh, I'm such a stupid ass. What am I doing here? What's the matter with me? I always have to do things the hard way. I knew this would happen. I knew this would happen.

MARTY: Look, will you stop bleeding all over my living room? You're not going to be a bride tonight, so forget it. If you wanted to get married so badly, why didn't you stay back in Ohio and marry the town square—or is it squire? You got in that chorus line. Nobody put you there.

JILL: I know. I know. The men there bore me, too. Along with my family and everybody else. I came here to find something better. What do I get?

MARTY: Me! Right?

JILL: Ohhhh . . . [*Is crying again.*]

MARTY: Oh, Christ. I said the wrong thing. . . . [*JILL continues crying.*] I give up. . . . [*She continues to cry, whimper, while* MARTY *goes to the bar to make a drink. He takes bottle, looks into bucket, finds no ice.*] Ahhhh . . . [*He picks up bucket and starts out of the living room.*] Don't go away. [*JILL continues to cry . . . and cry . . . She reaches down and pulls the twenty-dollar bill from her dress, unrolls it, looks at it. What to do with it? Cries . . . and cries . . . and rises . . . and walks over to her pocketbook, opens it, puts the money inside, closes it. Cries and cries . . . walks back to the couch, sits and continues crying.* MARTY *enters with ice bucket and some envelopes in his hands.*] Still going strong? I thought you might sneak out on me. . . . No? [*Makes his drink.*] No? [*Comes down to couch.* JILL *is letting up and has all but stopped.*]

JILL: I'm sorry—I'm such a child.

MARTY: Well, you said it. There now, wouldn't you like to help me read my mail? Just picked it up in the hall. Here you go. Hmmm? [*Handling a market paper.*] Gristede's is having a big sale. Need any Bartlett pears? Three cans for 87 cents. How are your loin center-cut pork chops? They are giving them away. Eh. . . . [*Puts it aside.*] Let's see . . . "Keep the Christmas spirit." "Buy Christmas Seals." Want some of these? Very colorful . . . No?

JILL: How come you don't have your own apartment?

MARTY: Hmm?

JILL: How come you don't have your own apartment?

MARTY: What kind of a question is that?

JILL: I'm just curious. You live with your folks out here. Couldn't you have your own place?

MARTY: I don't want my apartment.

JILL: Oh.

MARTY: I don't want my apartment! If you had all this, what would you want some little box for?

JILL: I wouldn't . . . but—if I were a man—it would be difficult.

MARTY: Sister, I couldn't tell you how many young lovelies spent the night in this place. I once had a chick in my room for two days and nobody knew about it. I threw the maid ten bucks, she cleaned around her, brought food up. I used to have breakfast with my old man and have it again with her. I once had a girl in my room—I went to work and she wandered around upstairs—washed her hair, used my mother's dryer— her bubble bath—went in and out of the refrigerator. My mother, here the whole time, didn't ask who she was. She knew. What the hell.

JILL: I shouldn't have washed my hair.

MARTY: Who are you kidding?

JILL: I don't know. Who are you kidding?

MARTY: I don't kid, sweetheart. I don't want to get married. I want to play around. I'm not kidding anybody. I'll tell you something. I was almost going to take a hotel room for you. That's another thing. If I don't want to come out here—I take a room. But I thought you'd like all this. . . .

JILL: What hotel?

MARTY: Ppfff—Come on. Now you're going to corner me on the couch—ask to go there and we start all over again. Just keep crying, baby. Ohhh . . . little postcard from my mother. Isn't it lovely? That's the dining room at the Fontainbleau. "Hello, Marty . . . Weather good, card game so so. Sending home Spanish tray I found. Aunt Minnie says hello." Well, isn't that exciting. A great big hello from Aunt Minnie. Ooop, what's this? [*Letter.*] What??? [*Opens it quickly.*]

JILL: Your hotel bill?

MARTY: Very funny . . . [*Rips it open and reads.*] Oh, for Christ sake!! Oh, for *Christ* sake!!! What's going on here??? [*He is up and waving the letter around in disbelief.*] What the hell is this???

JILL: What's the matter?

MARTY: Do you know what this is? Do—you—know—what —this—is??

JILL: No, what is it?

MARTY: It's my draft notice. This is my draft notice!!! That's impossible. That's goddammed impossible!! Do you know that?? Do you know that??

JILL: No, I don't.

MARTY: My old man already took care of this, goddam it. I'm 4F and working in a vital occupation and all the other crap that you have to be to get out of the army. My old man took care of that. Now what the hell's this??

JILL: Maybe he didn't take care of it.

MARTY: My old man took care of it. What the hell is this? Shit—I'll wake him up. [*Goes toward exit.*]

JILL: Marty, don't wake him now.

MARTY: Do you know what the hell this means? This means I'm supposed to go in the army. Somebody screwed up . . .

JILL: Nothing can be done until morning.

MARTY: You think I could sleep? [*Screaming upstairs.*] HEY . . . Dad! . . . Dad! . . . Goddam it . . . Dad! I'll be right back. [*Goes upstairs.*] Dad . . . Dad . . . [*JILL looks around, goes to bookshelf and begins examining books. We hear commotion upstairs, of MARTY waking his father, of father grumbling. Offstage:*] Come on . . . Come on the hell down . . . I want to find out what's coming off.

DAD [*Offstage*]:   You'll wake the whole neighborhood.

MARTY [*Offstage*]:   Then come on down. Somebody screwed up.

DAD [*Offstage*]:   Can't we do this in the morning?

MARTY [*Offstage*]:   Dad, I'm not going to sleep until I find out what happened.

DAD [*Offstage*]:   You can't wake up the whole armed forces.

MARTY [*Offstage*]:   Will you come downstairs???

DAD [*Offstage*]:   All right, all right. I'll be right down.

[MARTY *clumps down the stairs, reenters. Sees* JILL *at shelf.*]

MARTY: Find anything you like?

JILL: Oh . . . ah . . . don't you think I'd better go?

MARTY: That's all right. This won't take long. I just want to find what happened. How are you going to get home anyway?

JILL: I'll take a cab.

MARTY: It's cold out there. It's raining. You want to freeze your pretty little tail? You gonna swim home?

JILL: Can't you call one?

MARTY: Baby, it's three in the morning. You can't call a cab in *Manhattan* at three in the morning. Chrrrrist! [*Bangs on table.*]

JILL: What's the matter?

MARTY: Ahhh, maybe they sent it to the wrong guy. You think there's another Marty Gillman in the world? Some healthy-looking kid with no influence—huh?

JILL: Marty, if you and your father are going to talk . . .

MARTY: We're just going to talk, for God's sake. Don't worry, you'll be the first to know if there's going to be violence.

JILL: Isn't this a private matter?

MARTY: Look, if you want—go sit in the john. We've got towels in there with New Yorker cartoons on them. Keep yourself amused.

[MR. GILLMAN *enters.*]

DAD: All right, Marty. What's all the nonsense?

MARTY: This!! This—nonsense. [*Hands him letter.*]

DAD [*To* JILL]:   I'm sorry for the disturbance.

JILL: Oh, that's all right. Am I going to disturb you?

MARTY: Dad, will you please look at this thing.

DAD: Marty, you've got a guest here. Don't you think we could discuss this some other time?

MARTY: Look, how long is it going to take? Jill doesn't mind —it won't take a second.

DAD [*To* JILL]: I don't like to barge in like this—really.

JILL: It's perfectly all right. We were just—I mean if it's important.

MARTY: Barging? I *asked* you to come down.

JILL: Marty, maybe he does want to speak to you alone.

MARTY: Nobody has to go anywhere. The party can go on. You can go back to bed—just tell me what that is all about.

DAD: Get me a little drink, Marty—Cointreau.

MARTY: Uhhhhh [*Exasperated.*] . . . How about you, cookie?

JILL: No, I'm fine.

DAD: Did you ever have Cointreau? It's very good. Kind of orange flavor. Pour a little bit for Jill, Marty.

JILL: Well, I'll try it. Mr. Gillman?

DAD: Yes?

JILL: Did you collect all these books?

DAD: Oh—no—Most of them belonged to my brother. He was a college professor. He died of tuberculosis in some damn girls' college up in Maine or New Hampshire. They shipped all these books down here. He read em all. I'll tell you that. Some good books in there.

JILL: Yes . . . You have a—[*She goes to book.*] This is really signed by Fitzgerald?

DAD [*Looks at it*]: Ahhh . . . Yeah. That's what it says. There's one here signed by—Who's that other one signed by, Marty?

MARTY: God. We have a copy of the Bible signed by God.

DAD: What's the other signed thing, Marty?

MARTY: Eugene O'Neill.

DAD: Yeah, there's a book with Eugene O'Neill's name in it.

JILL [*Fitzgerald book*]:   That is such a lovely thing.

DAD: Yeah . . . well . . . he had a lot of them. [*Hands the book back.* MARTY *hands him a drink.*] All right—let's get this thing over with. I want to go to bed.

MARTY: You've got the letter. Read it.

DAD [*Reads*]:   Well?

MARTY: You must be kidding. That thing says I'm drafted. I'm supposed to report to active duty in another month.

DAD: I see that.

MARTY: Come on now—stop playing around, Buddy. What happened?

DAD: Very obviously, you were drafted.

MARTY: Will you stop that. It's a vaudeville routine. Look, what happened with everything you were going to take care of? Remember? [*To* JILL:] When I got the notice for the physical he said—"Take the physical. I'll talk to the congressman. I'll get the doctor to fix something up." [*To* DAD:] What happened to all that? You just forget?

DAD: No, I didn't forget.

MARTY: Dad, it's me, Marty—your son, your golf partner. Will you please play straight? Tell me what the letter is. If it's a mistake, all right.

DAD: Obviously someone made a mistake.

MARTY: That's all I want to know. Did obviously someone make a mistake—or . . .

DAD: Or what?

MARTY: . . . or you screwed up.

DAD: Or . . .

MARTY: Or what—what else could it be?

DAD: Or maybe I wanted you to be drafted.

MARTY: What???? Look, I didn't ask you to come down here to keep me up. I want you to tell me the truth so I can sleep tonight.

DAD: Well . . . that's the truth.

MARTY: What's the truth?

DAD: I . . . wanted you to be drafted.

MARTY [*Stands, looks*]:   Don't fuck around like that, old man. [JILL *rises on the obscenity and starts out.*] Where are you going?

JILL: Marty, this is none of my business.

MARTY: You stay here. I want someone to hear all this. Come on, sit over here. . . . Good. Sit—Listen—and drink your orange juice. . . . Good. [MR. GILLMAN *starts out.*] Where are *you* going?

DAD: I don't want to disturb you two any longer. You've found out what you wanted.

MARTY: What is the matter with you? Is Mother sitting on your head? I wanted to be drafted. Thank you. And good night.

DAD: Good night.

MARTY: Come on now, seriously. What is this??

DAD: Seriously, you got your draft notice, and I think it is a very good idea that you are going in the army. Now, need we discuss this further?

MARTY: Yes, we need do that! Now come on, old buddy!

DAD: You don't think that two years in the army might not do you some good?

MARTY: Good schmood. What am I, a juvenile delinquent?

DAD: Marty, please . . . I want you to get as much experience as possible. The army is an experience.

MARTY: You've been reading posters in the subway. Yeah, the army is an experience. A goddam miserable experience.

DAD: A little discipline never hurt anyone.

MARTY: Dad—[*To* JILL:] Do you believe it? In ninth grade—in ninth grade—I was flunking algebra—I wanted to drop the whole course. He says to me, "Mathematics is good for you. It's discipline—discipline never hurt anyone." Now you tell me—When the hell have I ever used algebra since ninth grade??

DAD: That's right—and when have you ever used the discipline?

MARTY [*Absolutely frustrated*]:   What . . . what . . . am I late to work? I don't do enough? I don't shine my shoes? I don't handle things when you're away? . . . what . . . what do I need . . . ?

DAD: Humility.

MARTY: WHAT IS THIS?? Arthur Godfrey Time? Dad, you're talking to me—*Me*. Yesterday, we were looking at skin flicks together in the den.

DAD: Marty, I want you to go into the army, because I think that the two years there can make you . . . And I think— you'll be that much better for it.

MARTY: Who wants to be better for it?

DAD: You should. That's the problem. . . . The army.

MARTY: What do you know about the army? What? You never got close to it. [*To* JILL:] You know where he was during the war? Big deal. He was an air raid warden. Learn a lot of discipline there, old man. Yeah, you tell me about the army.

DAD: If I could have gone in the army, I would have done it. I was too old. And—I had vital industry.

MARTY: I couldn't care less if you went in.

DAD: I wanted to go in.

MARTY: Ahhh. Come on. The war made you rich. What were you going to do in the army?

DAD: I don't know. I tried to join. You know that—I was too old.

MARTY: So now what? You want me to do it for you? Son gallantly lives the life the father never could. Well, if we're different—it's because—I *never* tried to join. I, in fact, have tried desperately to stay as far out of the army as is humanly possible. I am a very sick boy—and I am one who is invaluable to the paperbox industry.

DAD: What is so wrong with my wanting you to do what I couldn't do?

MARTY: Because I don't want to do what you couldn't do. Even if you could have done it, I don't want to do it. Even if you were now a four-star general, I still wouldn't want to do it. Is that clear? And furthermore, my doing won't give *you* the experience. It'll give me the experience. And *I* don't want it. Right? Right. [*To* JILL:] Right, baby? Taking all this down? Read it back.

JILL: Marty, this doesn't sound like it's going to take just a minute.

MARTY: All right, five minutes. Sit tight.

DAD [*To* JILL]:   I'm really very sorry. Look. Now that I'm up, why don't I show you some of the rooms upstairs.

MARTY: Dad . . .

DAD: There's a fireplace in our bedroom, too.

MARTY: Dad . . .

JILL: Well, I'd love to see it—but if you're—I can wait.

MARTY [*Whistles, then whispers*]:   Dad—what are we going to do about this?

DAD: We aren't going to do anything. It's already been done.

MARTY [*To* JILL]:   You hear that?—The same son—who couldn't stay on *one* campus for *one* year—he wants to stay in one army for two years.

DAD: Yes. I'd like you to stay at something.

MARTY: I've lived in this house for twenty-five years. That's staying! Why the hell don't I have my own apartment? Why can't I have my own apartment?

DAD: I told you why.

MARTY: I'm twenty-five years old. I can't live by myself?

DAD: There's no need to—if you have a comfortable home.

MARTY: I would like to live by myself. That's a reason. I'd like not to answer to a Goddamn maid every time I walk out of the house.

DAD: Well, go get yourself an apartment.

MARTY: How can I get myself an apartment? You pay my salary. If I rent an apartment, you cut off my salary. How do

I pay for it? You want me to go to work for someone else? Like maybe I couldn't do that. It doesn't cost so much to live in the city. You're the one who wants to give the company to *me*. You're the one who wants to keep it alive. All I want is an apartment—a little box—my own.

DAD: You stay out here.

MARTY: Ahhhh . . . what is the matter with you? Why? Give me a reason? Why? Or is it like the army? "I just want you to have the experience of living with a cockamamie mother and an arrogant maid. That's an important experience." All right. I've had my basic training. Now I can get out of here. Right?

DAD: You come and go as you please here. There's no need to waste good money on another place.

MARTY: Two hundred bucks a month. Christ, that's petty cash.

DAD: To you . . . yes, to you.

MARTY: To you too. Ahhhhh . . . something's wrong. Something is wrong.

DAD: I'm going to bed, Marty. Jill, I'm sorry to have to renege on my offer.

MARTY: We're not finished. You don't seriously think we're finished.

DAD: Yes.

MARTY: You're going to fix that thing—right?

DAD: No.

MARTY: Dad . . . you're going to fix that thing. You're going to call that congressman. Right?

DAD: No.

MARTY: What is it? Did you talk to that congressman, huh? Did you talk to him? Huh?

DAD: I told you I didn't. I decided that I thought . . .

MARTY: You did! You did talk to him, didn't you? [*Escorting his father warmly back.*] Come on, Dad. You can tell me, you know that.

DAD: I told you.

MARTY: Dad, I can tell when you say "pass the salt" what kind of a day it's been. . . . So come on—tell me what's going on.

DAD: I did not speak to anyone. I let the army draft you.

JILL: Marty . . . maybe he's telling you the truth.

MARTY: Baby . . . please . . . he's *my* old man. You tried to get it fixed. But you couldn't. Right?

DAD: Goodnight, Marty.

MARTY: Dad—will you please admit that to me? You couldn't get it fixed, right? Just say yes or no. How the hell can I do anything about it, if I don't know what happened?

DAD: You said you know what happened. So . . .

MARTY: So *you* tell me . . . Dad . . . please . . .

DAD: You know.

MARTY: You tell me.

DAD: I told you.

MARTY: You couldn't fix it. [*Quietly:*] Dad?

DAD: All right, I couldn't fix it.

MARTY: Ooohhhh . . . sonofabitch. Why didn't you say that before? Why? Why?

DAD: Marty, I tried. . . . I'm sorry.

MARTY: I don't understand. I don't understand. What is it with all the pull you have? If you don't have it, you should have told me. I could have done it myself. I could have flunked the physical. I could have paid some asthmatic creep off the street to take the physical for me. Ahhhh, Dad, why did you do this?

DAD: I tried. . . . I'm sorry. I tried, but nothing could be done.

MARTY: How did you try?

DAD: I did everything I could. I talked to the doctor. But he said it was too dangerous to fix anything. I tried several congressmen. I wrote to my old friend in the Senate.

MARTY: Your old *friend*.

DAD: I did everything I could.

MARTY: Dad, if you did everything you could, I wouldn't be drafted.

DAD: What else can I say? [*To* JILL:] You tell him, you're prettier than I am.

MARTY: I've got to get out of this thing. Somebody tell me!!

DAD: I guess it isn't so easy.

MARTY: It's easy if you've got something—like pull—or push. . . .

DAD: Marty, things change. You don't know what I went through.

MARTY: I know what I'm *not* going through, and that is two years of playing soldier.

DAD: And what are you going to do, Marty?

MARTY: What am *I* going to do? . . . What *am* I going to do? Hey—[*Goes to* JILL.] You want to get married? Marry me. Come on. Marry me. We'll have a quick kid. They'll defer me. . . . Look—look, we don't even have to get married. All I have to do is have the kid. How about that?? . . . That's easy huh? Huh?

JILL: Marty, you're hurting my hand.

MARTY: I'm sorry—don't you want to get married?

JILL: Your father told you what happened already. I don't understand why you keep going.

MARTY: Baby, he screwed up. If he can't unscrew it with his pull, somebody's got to.

DAD: For the last time, Marty, I told you I tried. And I'm sorry.

MARTY: Dad, if you're so sorry, you report to Fort Dix on February third. And . . .

DAD: Marty, listen. Just listen to this, will you?

MARTY: Yeah? [*As* DAD *rattles this off,* MARTY *wanders distractedly around.*]

DAD: I told you, I wrote a letter to that senator. I called

the congressman. I told you I called him, but it's an election year. He's afraid to do anything that might reflect on his record, and after all, Marty—I'm not a big political buff. I haven't given a lot of money to the party. Politics works on a constituent basis. I mean I could be head of General Motors and if I don't give any money to the party, or swing a lot of votes, why nobody pays any attention . . .

[MARTY *is wandering, picking at furniture.* JILL *whispers loudly.*]

JILL: Marty . . . listen to him.

DAD: . . . to you. You know that, Marty. That's common sense. You can only get favors . . . when there's something to give for them. Now . . . I mean . . . during the war . . . I had a few favors . . . but I mean there was no competition . . . I mean it was cheap . . .

JILL: Marty . . .

MARTY: "During the war," I'm listening.

DAD: . . . a nice girl in town . . . that was a favor. . . . I mean, Marty, if it was like the old days, you could come in very handy. The women you know, Marty, but it's different now. I just don't know that many people in Washington . . . or Albany. . . . I mean money talks . . . but it depends on what you do with it. . . . I mean . . . even then I tried. . . . I wrote him a letter. . . . I called him . . . person to person. . . . He wrote back. . . . I'll show you the letter. Marty, do you want to see the letter? Marty?

MARTY: What?

DAD: What else can I tell you?

[JILL *is crying.*]

MARTY: What is the matter with you now?

JILL: I don't even know you. Why don't you listen to him, Marty? Maybe . . . maybe your father's right. I mean the army can be a valuable experience . . . I mean my cousin Roger went into the army and he was just a kid when he went in . . . and you should have seen him when he came out.

. . . I mean the time. . . . It changed him from . . . and I think your father may have a point there, Marty.

MARTY: What is it to you, huh? Why don't you just stay out of this?

JILL: I have been trying to. I've been trying to leave. But you won't let me. [*Still crying.*]

DAD: Why don't you take the girl home, Marty?

MARTY: I don't want to take the girl home. I invited her here. I don't want to take her home.

DAD: And you don't want to go in the army. And what else do you want?

MARTY: I want to get this damn thing straightened out. Are you going to stop crying?

JILL: Not until you take me home!

DAD: I'll take her home.

MARTY: The hell you will. Not while I'm eligible for the draft.

DAD: Just let me get dressed. I'll be right down.

JILL: All right. I'd appreciate that. I'm sorry.

MARTY [*Stops father*]:   Now just a minute. We haven't finished our little powwow.

DAD: I finished, Marty.

MARTY: You mean I'*m* finished.

DAD: I'll get dressed.

JILL: I'll wait.

MARTY: Now just a goddam minute. Is it all right if I join the party? OK, OK. We're going to make nice. All right, everybody's gonna be real civil. And we're going to make nice. [*Taking his father by the arm and escorting him to couch.*] And we're going to sit and chat and straighten out one thing at a time.

DAD: Marty . . . I want to get dressed . . . and take the young lady home . . . so I can get to bed.

MARTY: It's my young lady. I'll take her home. You worry about your problems. [*Seats him.*] Making me a civilian!

JILL: Marty . . . [*Teary again.*] Please . . . I'll take a cab.

MARTY: OK now . . . here's what we do. [*Picking up golf clubs.*] Here's what we do. We do this like sportsmen. I challenge you to five holes—five quick holes. If you win, I take Jillsie home, and we talk in the morning. If I win, we talk now . . . and she . . .

JILL: And what do I do?

MARTY: You can play too if you'd like. If you win—I'll give you the car. You can get home on your own steam.

JILL: I've had enough! Oh, for God's sake . . .

MARTY: Come on, Dad . . . [*Hands him a club.*] Big challenge match.

DAD: Marty, it's after three in the morning.

MARTY: That's the best time for golf. No one on the course. [DAD *takes golf club.*] Good . . . little match. [DAD *tosses it across the room.*] Heyyy—what's the matter? Don't you like the stakes? Dad . . . I'm serious. I'm trying to make nice. I really want to settle this thing. You said you're sorry. Prove it to me . . . convince me . . . tell me very quietly . . . and we'll sit here and figure out a way . . . that things can be straightened out. OK? We'll do our little straightening out routine. OK? You ready for the straightening-out routine, honey? Get in your costume . . . and—a one—two—three, four. [*Using club as a cane, he does soft shoe to the following, singing.*]

> Things are screwed up now, but they won't be long
> Da . . . da . . . da . . .
> Things are screwed up now, but they won't be long
> Da . . . da . . . da . . .

Come on, baby—grab a line. [*He puts his arm in hers and begins cancan.*] Show the old man how you do it. [*He begins humming cancan music and doing it, pulling her along.*]

Daaaaa . . . da da da da . . . da da . . . da dad dad . . .
come on.

JILL: Marty, I don't—Marty I can't . . . Marty . . .

DAD: Marty—you're going to wake the whole house up.

MARTY: She's very good at this . . . when she tries. . . .
Come on . . . Da . . . dad . . . dadda . . .

JILL [*Tears away*]:   Marty!!

MARTY: Come on, baby. The old man never saw you do your
stuff. She's very good. She really is. And the amazing thing
is—there are four thousand girls in that line. . . . They all
look alike from the balcony. All except for Jill. There is something about the way she kicks—right? Show him. [*He does
one.*] Ta . . . daaa!!!

DAD: Marty, I'm going to get you the letter. [*Exits to go upstairs.*]

MARTY: What? Where you—? What letter? [*Starts after* DAD,
Comes back in. Going to her.] Look—do me a little favor,
huh? How about it? The old man likes you. He thinks you're
cute. Why don't you do a few steps for him? It wouldn't kill
you.

JILL: What in God's name for, Marty? I . . .

MARTY: For me, baby. Something is wrong with the old man.
Something is bugging him. I don't know what to believe. I
just want to loosen him up, you know. If he's enjoying himself
he'll play straight with me. I don't know what's wrong with
him. Maybe the old lady's on his neck.

JILL: Maybe it's you, Marty.

MARTY [*Mimics her*]:   "Maybe it's you, Marty." Look, will
you do me a favor, for Christ sake. It won't kill you—just . . .
some of that Christmas spirit, you know.

JILL: And then you take me home?

MARTY: I promise. You know—just a little bit. . . . I promise I'll take you home.

JILL: I know your promises.

MARTY: Come on, I'm just asking a little favor. I don't want you to take anything off. Just make some noise. Kick. Please, please, baby.

DAD [*Enters with letter in his hand*]:   Here you are, Marty— It's from the congressman.

MARTY [*Takes it, ignoring it. Leads* JILL *in front of couch*]: All right, Dad. We've got a little treat for you.

JILL: Marty, please. I'd rather not.

DAD: Marty, aren't you going to read the letter?

MARTY: Yeah, I'm going to read it. I want you to see something first. Look—everybody's getting a little upset. We're going to make nice a little . . . have a good time . . . and talk sensibly. Right? And the pride of Ohio here is going to do a little Santa Claus rag . . . just for you, Dad . . . she likes your smile.

JILL [*Whispers*]:   I never said that . . .

MARTY: Come on, honey—please. Here we go, Pop. Little fun before business.

DAD: Marty, I'm really not in the mood.

MARTY: That's the point. That—is—the—point! Yeahhhh here we go . . . [*Whispers.*] No music. Just sing something Christmas.

JILL: Rockettes don't sing.

MARTY: Sing something Christmas. You know—Santa Claus . . . [*To* DAD:] She sings too. . . . Here we go . . . a one . . . a two . . . a three . . . a four . . .

JILL [*Just stands, turns meekly to* MR. GILLMAN]:   Rockettes don't sing usually.

MARTY: And one . . . a two . . . a three . . . a four. Come on. . . . "Better watch out. Better not cry." . . . You know that . . . one . . . two . . . three . . . and [JILL *begins singing, doing kicks.* MARTY *sings with her.*]

JILL and MARTY:
> Better watch out,
> Better not cry,
> Better not pout,

> *I'm telling you why.*
> *Santa Claus is coming*
> *To town.*

MARTY: Two, three, four . . . one, two, three, four.

JILL [*Alone now*]:

> *He's makin' a list,*
> *Checkin' it twice,*
> *Gonna find out who's*
> *Naughty or nice.*
> *Santa Claus is coming to town*

[*She becomes teary now as she sings.*]

> *He knows when you are sleeping,*
> *He knows when you're awake,*
> *He knows when you are good,*
> *Or bad,*
> *So be good*
> *For goodness sake.*

[*She stands now, just crying. She cries and cries and cries and . . . slowly she stops, lifts her head, looks, quietly.*]

> *I wish you a merry Christmas,*
> *I wish you a merry Christmas,*
> *I wish you a merry Christmas,*
> *And a happy New Year.*

That's my solo. [*She walks to couch and sits.*]

MARTY [*Applauds*]:   Very nice. Very nice. Heyyy, Pop—pull out the projector and we'll show the feature. How about a little *What Price Glory?*, *Sands of Iwo Jima*, *Pork Chop Hill*, a few films about how much fun the army is—all that wonderful experience. Huh? Huh?

DAD: Read the letter, Marty.

MARTY [*Looks at him, her, takes it, reads*]:   "Office of Congressman Richard Fuller, Capitol, Washington. Dear Mr. Gillman. I'm sorry to" uh huh . . . uh huh . . . [*Reads silently. Finishes. Looks up.*] Dear Mr. Gillman, who the hell are you? Right?

DAD: Right.

MARTY [*Holding back steam, walks, walks*]:   My buddy. There's my buddy over there, fans. I could have gotten . . . I could have gotten out of this *myself!* There is a little form you fill out. They ask you questions. Are you a homosexual? Yes! Do you wet your bed? Yes! Did you ever take dope? Yes! Pardon me, sergeant, I'm late for my fix! Why didn't you tell me at first? Just tell me you couldn't swing it and say, Marty . . . do it *yourself*.

DAD: You know what you would have done if I'd said that.

MARTY: I'd have respected that.

DAD: You'd have kicked and screamed all over this house!

MARTY: My ass.

DAD: You'd have kicked and screamed all over this house. Your mother was in Miami, remember? The day we finished the golf game, and . . . you said you deserved a prize for winning, and I was going to buy you a bottle. You wanted a car. You wanted a sportscar. And did you get it? No sleep. We went right down for the car. I'm a poor loser . . . after three days without sleep. I can't take you when you want something. You want too loud. All I ask from your mother and you is company. Yeah, Marty. Sometimes you give me that. Yeah, Marty, we're buddies. That what you want? OK. I'm sorry I couldn't get you out . . . but . . . I thought you would appreciate my attempt. And you didn't.

MARTY: What? Show me something to appreciate. This letter? Yeah—I appreciate this. [*Rips it up and throws it into the air.*] Happy New Year. [*Points to paper.*] Police the area . . . Private!

DAD: Thanks, Marty. Thank you, Marty. I didn't try hard
enough. What more can I give you? What more? I only ever
asked one thing of you and your mother, goddam it. Appreciation. Your mother forgot that years ago. She takes . . .
and never blinks an eye . . . and I couldn't care less. You
want, Marty. Fine. You're my buddy, Marty . . . fine. . . .
But don't tell me, Marty, that I didn't try. You are all I've
ever had Marty . . . so don't you dare . . . tell me I didn't
try . . . Buddy.

MARTY: Oh . . . come on, come on. I appreciate . . . I appreciate. What's the matter with *me?* What is the matter
with wanting what I want? You know what happens when you
stop wanting? You stop getting! That's right. You stop getting. What do you want? Name a few thousand things. . . .
You wanted this place. You got it. You wanted a six-figure
income. You got it! You wanted my mother. You got her!
What you want you get. Right? Right. Jillsie. Tell us. What
do you want? Go on, tell me what do you want? [*Goes to
bookshelves.*] You want some of these? You want some of
these books? Very classy books. Well, ask. Just ask. Say,
"Gosh I'd like some of those books." Go ahead. [*He brings
a handful to her.*]

JILL: Marty . . . I . . . I'm . . .

MARTY: Go ahead. "Gosh Marty, I'd like some of those
books . . ."

JILL: Marty, put them back. They're very valuable.

MARTY: Put 'em back? But you want them. Right? You told
me. You want them, right? Well, damn it, get what you want.
[*He runs to shelf, comes with a pile and drops them on couch
with others. And goes back for more.*] If you want something,
you ask. Then, if you can't get it—take it . . . as long as it's
legal . . . take it . . . right???

DAD: Marty, take it easy—there's some valuable books.

MARTY: How would you know? Here, baby—you want, you
got. [*Piles books on couch around* JILL. JILL *finally gets up
and intercepts* MARTY *coming with a handful.*]

JILL: Marty, please . . . don't. . . . They're . . . you'll ruin
them, Marty.

[MARTY *wrestles to get away from her and the books drop on
floor.*]

MARTY: Look what you did.

JILL: Oh, Marty. [*She bends to pick them up.*]

MARTY: I thought you wanted them. Look what you did.

JILL [*Gets up facing* MARTY]:   I wanted them! I wanted what!
I wanted what, Marty? All I wanted about an hour ago was
for you to take me home. That's all. That's not asking much.
You want to give everybody what they want. Why don't you
give some little things first—little hard things. You want . . .
you want . . . how about what other people want? What
they *really* want? Somehow you turn off when those requests
are made. Somehow you turn off.

MARTY: So cry again. So cry again and tell me you want to
get married. Tell me that. Tell me how much you want that.
Hah hah! Guilty. Guilty. How desperate are you? Huh? You
want to get married so bad? You didn't mind going out with
me, did you? You wanted enough to take that on. Sister, if
you wanted to leave, you could have left anytime tonight.
Back in the city. Back in the cloakroom, back in the club.
Why didn't you leave me then? You wait till we're out in
hell and gone and then you want to leave. When it's difficult,
when you can say "I can't leave," when it's my fault for not
taking you. Well, sister, you could have even left here. Oh, it
might have been hard—a cab ride—but I'm a Goddam good
prospect for a girl from Ohio. I'm quite a catch. Right? All
the time you sit here saying to yourself, "He's a big, loud slob
. . . but . . . maybe he's drunk. Maybe he's different later
on. Maybe you get used to it. Maybe he's just trying to im-
press me . . . and later on . . . he becomes the real Marty
Gillman . . . humble and full of loving kindness toward
wandering chorus girls. He's a catch. It's worth waiting. Just
a minute more, just a minute . . . more. . . . I can cry.
. . . I can still cry. . . . He might wilt if I cry. He might be

tender—might, might, might." Well, Chicken Pie? Are you ready to marry me?? You ready to tell me about what you want? I know, baby—You'll leave when you want. . . . And *here* you *are!!!* [*He walks away from her.* JILL *again begins to cry. Stops herself. Picks up the books and takes them back to the shelf, then crosses to where her coat is on the chair, and starts to put it on.*]

DAD: I'll take you home, my dear.

JILL: I've heard that.

DAD: No. I'll just put a coat on top of my pajamas. Please wait. [*He exits.*]

MARTY: Wait . . . here . . . [*He goes to shelf, shuffles through books.*] Here's a present for you. [*Goes to her.*] Take this one at least. It's the Fitzgerald.

JILL: That's not yours to give.

[DAD *enters.*]

MARTY: Dad . . . she likes this book.

JILL: No . . .

DAD [*Walks over and takes it*]:   What is it? . . . Oh?

MARTY: Give it to her.

JILL: I don't want it.

MARTY: You don't *want* it. Shit . . . [*Takes it from his father and shoves it in her hand.*] Here. . . . Go home . . .

JILL: I don't want it now! You think I stayed around for this! That's what you think. You think I can't find another Fitzgerald. Well I know someone who has a *Bernard Shaw!!* [*She parades all the way across to the bookshelf. Plunks it down. Parades back.*] Take me home!!

DAD: I'll be back late.

MARTY: I know how long it takes. Have a nice ride. I'll be up. We still have a talk. Remember?

DAD: Marty, I want to tell you something.

MARTY: Whaaaat?

DAD: Nothing.

MARTY: What . . . what is it?

DAD: I'm sorry I lied to you, Marty. But I can't get everything I want.

MARTY: You didn't want it enough.

DAD: Fortunately for both of us.

MARTY: Ohhh . . . that's funny. That's very funny. Thank you Morey Amsterdam. But I am not going into your army.

DAD: We'll see. Night, Marty. [*A faint salute, and he exits.*]

MARTY [*Looks after him. Then quietly, self-assuredly, to himself*]:   Yeah . . . we'll see. We'll see if I'm going to have some nigger sergeant tell me when to get up in the morning. . . . I'm not going to wait in line for a tray. [*Chuckles.*] March around like an idiot with a toy gun . . . heh . . . On February third, I will be right here—right? Right. I'll tell all the generals to go screw themselves. . . . Yeah . . . I'll wet my bed—right? . . . I'll wet every damn sheet in the army till they let me out—right? . . . The President himself can come up here. He can get down on his knees . . . and plead. . . . I'll be damned if I go—rrright? [*Offstage the door slams.*] Rrrright. [MARTY *picks up golf club.*] Just 'cause the old man wasn't smart enough . . . heh . . . we'll see who's smart. . . . [*We hear the gravel fly and the car pull away.* MARTY *stands with the club, listens, listens as the sound disappears. He fingers the club, grips it, into a swinging position, grips it, listens. It is quiet . . . then he beats the club violently on the back of the couch and screams.*] I—won't go!! I REFUSE TO GO!! THAT'S FINAL. THAT'S FINAL!! I WON'T GO. I WON'T—I WON'T—I WON'T—I WON'T. . . .

CURTAIN

Dutchman) *what title do signify?*

LeRoi Jones

CAST:

white Lula .... Jennifer West

black Clay .... Robert Hooks

Directed by Edward Parone

First presented at Cherry Lane Theatre, March 24, 1964.
Produced by Theater 1964 (Richard Barr,
Clinton Wilder, Edward Albee).

SCENE: *In the flying underbelly of the city. Steaming hot, and*
summer on top, outside. Underground. The subway
heaped in modern myth.

People in the Play:

CLAY, a 20-year-old Negro
LULA, a 30-year-old white woman
YOUNG NEGRO
CONDUCTOR
Riders of coach (white and black)

SCENE I

Opening scene is a man sitting in a subway seat, holding a magazine, but looking vacantly just above its wilting pages. Occasionally he looks blankly toward the window on his right. Dim lights and darkness whistling by against the glass. (Or paste the lights, as admitted props, right on the subway windows. Have them move, even dim and flicker. But give the sense of speed. Also stations, whether the train is stopped or the glitter and activity of these stations merely flashes by the windows.)

The man is sitting alone. That is, only his seat is visible. Though the rest of the car is outfitted as a complete subway car. But only his seat is shown. There might be, for a time, as the play begins, a loud scream of the actual train. And it can recur wherever, throughout the play, or continue on a lower key once the dialogue starts.

The train slows after a time, pulling to a brief stop at one of the stations. The man looks idly up, until he sees a woman's face staring at him through the window, which, when it realizes that the man has noticed it, begins very premeditatedly to smile. The man smiles too, for a moment, without a trace of self-consciousness. Almost an instinctive though undesirable response. Then a kind of awkwardness sets in, or embarrassment, and the man makes to look away, is further embarrassed, so he brings back his eyes to where the face was, but by now the train is moving again, and the face would seem to be left behind by the way the man turns his head to look back through the other windows at the slowly fading platform. He smiles then, more comfortably confident, hoping perhaps that his memory of this brief encounter will be pleasant. And then he is idle again.

   Train roars. Lights flash outside the windows.

   LULA *enters from the rear of the car in bright, skimpy summer clothes and sandals. She carries a net bag full of paper books, fruit, and other anonymous articles. She is wearing sunglasses, which she pushes up on her forehead from time to time.* LULA *is a tall, slender, beautiful woman with long red hair hanging straight down her back, wearing only loud lipstick in somebody's good taste. She is eating an apple, very daintily. Coming down the car towards* CLAY.

   She stops beside CLAY's *seat, and hangs languidly from the strap, still managing to eat the apple. It is apparent that she is going to sit in the seat next to* CLAY, *and that she is only waiting for him to notice her before she sits.*

   CLAY *sits as before, looking just beyond his magazine, now and again pulling the magazine slowly back and forth in front of his face in a hopeless effort to fan himself. Then he sees the woman hanging there beside him, and he looks up into her face, smiling quizzically.*

LULA: Hello.

CLAY: Uh, hi're you?

LULA: I'm going to sit down—OK?

CLAY: Sure.

LULA [*Swings down onto the seat, pushing her legs straight out as if she is very weary*]:   Oooof! Too much weight.

CLAY: Ha, doesn't look like much to me. [*Leaning back against the window, a little surprised and maybe stiff.*]

LULA: It's so anyway. [*And she moves her toes in the sandals, then pulls her right leg up on the left knee better to inspect the bottoms of the sandals and the back of her heel. She appears for a second not to notice that* CLAY *is sitting next to her, or that she has spoken to him just a second before.* CLAY *looks at the magazine, then out the black window.*

As he does this, she turns very quickly toward him.] Weren't
you staring at me through the window?

CLAY [*Wheeling around and very much stiffened*]:   What?

LULA: Weren't you staring at me through the window? At
the last stop?

CLAY: Staring at you? What do you mean?

LULA: Don't you know what "staring" means?

CLAY: I saw you through the window—if that's what it
means. I don't know if I was staring. Seems to me you were
staring through the window at me.

LULA: I was. But only after I'd turned around and saw you
staring through that window down in the vicinity of my ass
and legs.

CLAY: Really?

LULA: Really. I guess you were just taking those idle pot-
shots. Nothing else to do. Run your mind over people's flesh.

CLAY: Oh, boy. Wow, now I admit I was looking in your
direction. But the rest of that weight is yours.

LULA: I suppose.

CLAY: Staring through train windows is weird business. Much
weirder than staring very sedately at abstract asses.

LULA: That's why I came looking through the window—so
you'd have more than that to go on. I even smiled at you.

CLAY: That's right.

LULA: I even got into this train, going some other way than
mine. Walked down the aisle . . . searching you out.

CLAY: Really? That's pretty funny.

LULA: That's pretty funny—God, you're dull.

CLAY: Well, I'm sorry, lady, but I really wasn't prepared for
party talk.

LULA: No, you're not. What are you prepared for? [*Wrap-
ping the apple core in a kleenex and dropping it on the floor.*]

CLAY [*Takes her conversation as pure sex talk. He turns to con-
front her squarely with this idea*]:   I'm prepared for anything. How about you?

LULA [*Laughing loudly and cutting it off abruptly*]:   What
do you think you're doing?

CLAY: What?

LULA: You think I want to pick you up, get you to take me
somewhere and screw me, huh?

CLAY: Is that the way I look?

LULA: You look like you been trying to grow a beard. That's
exactly what you look like. You look like you live in New
Jersey with your parents and are trying to grow a beard.
That's what. You look like you've been reading Chinese poetry
and drinking lukewarm sugarless tea. [*Laughs, uncrossing and
recrossing her legs.*] You look like death eating a soda cracker.

CLAY [*Cocking his head from one side to the other, embarrassed
and trying to make some comeback, but also intrigued by
what the woman is saying . . . even the sharp city coarseness
of her voice, which is still a kind of gentle sidewalk throb*]:
Really? I look like all that?

LULA: Not all of it. [*She feints a seriousness to cover an
actual somber tone.*] I lie a lot. [*Smiling.*] It helps me control
the world.

CLAY [*Relieved and laughing louder than the humor*]:   Yeh,
I bet.

LULA: But it's true, most of it, right? Jersey? Your bumpy
neck?

CLAY: How'd you know all that? Huh? Really, I mean about
Jersey . . . and even the beard. I met you before? You know
Warren Enright?

LULA: You tried to make it with your sister when you were
ten. [CLAY *leans hard against the back of the seat, his eyes
opening now still trying to look amused.*] But I succeeded a
few weeks ago. [*She starts to laugh again.*]

CLAY: What're you talking about? Warren tell you that?
You're a friend of Georgia's?

LULA: I told you I lie. I don't know your sister. I don't know
Warren Enright.

CLAY: You mean you're just picking these things out of the air?

LULA: Is Warren Enright a tall, skinny, black black boy with a phoney English accent?

CLAY: I figured you knew him.

LULA: But I don't. I just figured you would know somebody like that. [*Laughs.*]

CLAY: Yeah, yeah.

LULA: You're probably on your way to his house now.

CLAY: That's right.

LULA [*Putting her hand on* CLAY's *closest knee, drawing it from the knee up to the thigh's hinge, then removing it, watching his face very closely, and continuing to laugh, perhaps more gently than before*]: Dull, dull, dull. I bet you think I'm exciting.

CLAY: You're OK.

LULA: Am I exciting you now?

CLAY: Right. That's not what's supposed to happen?

LULA: How do I know? [*She returns her hand, without moving it, then takes it away and plunges it in her bag to draw out an apple.*] You want this?

CLAY: Sure.

LULA [*She gets one out of the bag for herself*]: Eating apples together is always the first step. Or walking up uninhabited Seventh Avenue in the Twenties on weekends. [*Bites and giggles, glancing at* CLAY *and speaking in loose sing-song.*] Can get you involved . . . boy! Get us involved. Umhuh. [*Mock seriousness.*] Would you like to get involved with me, Mister Man?

CLAY [*Trying to be as flippant as* LULA, *whacking happily at the apple*]: Sure. Why not? A beautiful woman like you. Huh, I'd be a fool not to.

LULA: And I bet you're sure you know what you're talking about. [*Taking him a little roughly by the wrist, so he cannot eat the apple, then shaking the wrist.*] I bet you're sure of

almost everything anybody ever asked you about—right?
[*Shakes his wrist harder.*] Right?

CLAY: Yeh, right . . . wow, you're pretty strong, you know?
Whatta you, a lady wrestler or something?

LULA: What's wrong with lady wrestlers? And don't answer
because you never knew any. Huh. [*Cynically.*] That's for
sure. They don't have any lady wrestlers in that part of Jersey. That's for sure.

CLAY: Hey, you still haven't told me how you know so much
about me.

LULA: I told you I didn't know anything about *you* . . .
you're a well-known type.

CLAY: Really?

LULA: Or at least I know the type very well. And your skinny
English friend too.

CLAY: Anonymously?

LULA [*Settles back in seat singlemindedly finishing her apple,
and humming snatches of rhythm and blues song*]:   What?

CLAY: Without knowing us specifically?

LULA: Oh, boy. [*Looking quickly at* CLAY.] What a face.
You know you could be a handsome man.

CLAY: I can't argue with you.

LULA [*Vague, off-center response*]:   What?

CLAY [*Raising his voice, thinking the train noise has drowned
part of his sentence*]:   I can't argue with you.

LULA: My hair is turning gray. A gray hair for each year and
type I've come through.

CLAY: Why do you want to sound so old?

LULA: But it's always gentle when it starts. [*Attention drifting.*] Hugged against tenements, day or night.

CLAY: What?

LULA [*Refocussing*]:   Hey, why don't you take me to that
party you're going to?

CLAY: You must be a friend of Warren's to know about the
party.

LULA: Wouldn't you like to take me to the party? [*Imitates clinging vine.*] Oh, come on, ask me to your party.

CLAY: Of course, I'll ask you to come with me to the party. And I'll bet you're a friend of Warren's.

LULA: Why not be a friend of Warren's? Why not? [*Taking his arm.*] Have you asked me yet?

CLAY: How can I ask you when I don't know your name?

LULA: Are you talking to my name?

CLAY: What is it, a secret?

LULA: I'm Lena the Hyena.

CLAY: The famous woman poet?

LULA: Poetess! The same!

CLAY: Well, you know so much about me . . . what's my name?

LULA: Morris the Hyena.

CLAY: The famous woman poet?

LULA: The same. [*Laughing and going into her bag.*] You want another apple?

CLAY: Can't make it, lady. I only have to keep one doctor away a day.

LULA: I bet your name is . . . something like . . . uh, Gerald or Walter. Huh?

CLAY: God, no.

LULA: Lloyd, Norman? One of those hopeless colored names creeping out of New Jersey. Leonard? Gag . . .

CLAY: Like Warren?

LULA: Definitely. Just exactly like Warren. Or Everett.

CLAY: Gag . . .

LULA: Well, for sure, it's not Willie.

CLAY: It's Clay.

LULA: Clay? Really? Clay what?

CLAY: Take your pick. Jackson, Johnson, or Williams.

LULA: Oh, really? Good for you. But it's got to be Williams. You're too pretentious to be a Jackson or Johnson.

CLAY: Thassright.

LULA: But Clay's OK.

CLAY: So's Lena.

LULA: It's Lula.

CLAY: Oh?

LULA: Lula the hyena.

CLAY: Very good.

LULA [*Starts laughing again*]:   Now you say to me, "Lula, Lula, why don't you go to this party with me tonight?" It's your turn, and let those be your lines.

CLAY: Lula, why don't you go to this party with me tonight? Huh?

LULA: Say my name twice before you ask, and no huh's.

CLAY: Lula, Lula, why don't you go to this party with me tonight?

LULA: I'd like to go, Clay, but how can you ask me to go when you barely know me?

CLAY: That is strange, isn't it?

LULA: What kind of reaction is that? You're supposed to say, "Aw, come on, we'll get to know each other better at the party."

CLAY: That's pretty corny.

LULA: What are you into anyway? [*Looking at him half-sullenly but still amused.*] What thing are you playing at, Mister? Mister Clay Williams? [*Grabs his thigh, up near the crotch.*] What are *you* thinking about?

CLAY: Watch it now, you're gonna excite me for real.

LULA [*Taking her hand away, and throwing her apple core through the window*]:   I bet. [*She slumps in the seat and is heavily silent.*]

CLAY: I thought you knew everything about me? What happened? [LULA *looks at him, then looks slowly away, then over where the other aisle would be. Noise of the train. She reaches in her bag and pulls out one of the paper books. She puts it on her leg and thumbs the pages listlessly.* CLAY *cocks his head to see the title of the book. Noise of the train.* LULA

flips pages and her eyes drift. Both remain silent.] Are you
going to the party with me, Lula?

LULA [*Bored and not even looking*]:   I don't even know you.

CLAY: You said you know my type.

LULA [*Strangely irritated*]:   Don't get smart with me, Buster.
I know you like the palm of my hand.

CLAY: The one you eat the apples with?

LULA: Yeh. And the one I open doors late Saturday eve-
ning with. That's my door. Up at the top of the stairs. Five
flights. Above a lot of Italians, and lying Americans. And
scrape carrots with. Also . . . [*Looks at him.*] the same hand
I unbutton my dress with, or let my skirt fall down. Same
hand. Lover.

CLAY: Are you angry about something? Did I say something
wrong?

LULA: Everything you say is wrong. [*Mock smile.*] That's
what makes you so attractive. Ha. In that funnybook jacket
with all the buttons. [*More animate, taking hold of his jacket.*]
What've you got that jacket and tie on in all this heat for?
And why're you wearing a jacket and tie like that? Did your
people ever burn witches or start revolutions over the price
of tea? Boy, those narrow shoulder clothes come from a tradi-
tion you ought to feel oppressed by. A three-button suit. What
right do you have to be wearing a three-button suit and
striped tie? Your grandfather was a slave, he didn't go to
Harvard.

CLAY: My grandfather was a night watchman.

LULA: And you went to a colored college where everybody
thought they were Averell Harriman.

CLAY: All except me.

LULA: And who did you think you were? Who do you think
you are now?

CLAY [*Laughs as if to make light of the whole trend of the conversation*]:   Well, in college I thought I was Baudelaire.
But I've slowed down since.

LULA: I bet you never once thought you were a black nigger. [*Mock serious, then she howls with laughter.* CLAY *is stunned but after initial reaction, he quickly tries to appreciate the humor.* LULA *almost shrieks.*] A black Baudelaire.

CLAY: That's right.

LULA: Boy, are you corny. I take back what I said before. Everything you say is not wrong. It's perfect. You should be on television.

CLAY: You act like you're on television already.

LULA: That's because I'm an actress.

CLAY: I thought so.

LULA: Well, you're wrong. I'm no actress. I told you I always lie. I'm nothing, honey, and don't you ever forget it. [*Lighter.*] Although my mother was a Communist. The only person in my family ever to amount to anything.

CLAY: My mother was a Republican.

LULA: And your father voted for the man rather than the party.

CLAY: Right!

LULA: Yea for him. Yea, yea for him.

CLAY: Yea!

LULA: And yea for America where he is free to vote for the mediocrity of his choice! Yea!

CLAY: Yea!

LULA: And yea for both your parents who, even though they differ about so crucial a matter as the body politic, still forged a union of love and sacrifice that was destined to flower at the birth of the noble Clay—what's your middle name?

CLAY: Clay.

LULA: A union of love and sacrifice that was destined to flower at the birth of the noble Clay Clay Williams. Yea! And most of all yea yea for you, Clay Clay. The Black Baudelaire! Yes! [*And with knifelike cynicism.*] My Christ. My Christ.

CLAY: Thank you, ma'm.

LULA: May the people accept you as a ghost of the future. And love you, that you might not kill them when you can.

CLAY: What?

LULA: You're a murderer, Clay, and you know it. [*Her voice darkening with significance.*] You know goddam well what I mean.

CLAY: I do?

LULA: So we'll pretend the air is light and full of perfume.

CLAY [*Sniffing at her blouse*]:   It is.

LULA: And we'll pretend the people cannot see you. That is, the citizens. And that you are free of your own history. And I am free of my history. We'll pretend that we are both anonymous beauties smashing along through the city's entrails. [*She yells as loud as she can.*] GROOVE!

BLACKOUT

SCENE II

Scene is the same as before, though now there are other seats visible in the car. And throughout the scene other people get on the subway. There are maybe one or two seated in the car as the scene opens, though neither CLAY nor LULA notices them. CLAY's tie is open. LULA is hugging his arm.

CLAY: The party!

LULA: I know it'll be something good. You can come in with me, looking casual and significant. I'll be strange, haughty and silent, and walk with long slow strides.

CLAY: Right.

LULA: When you get drunk, pat me once, very lovingly, on the flanks, and I'll look at you cryptically, licking my lips.

CLAY: It sounds like something we can do.

LULA: You'll go around talking to young men about your mind, and to old men about your plans. If you meet a very close friend who is also with someone like me, we can stand together, sipping our drinks and exchanging codes of lust. The atmosphere will be slithering in love and half-love and very open moral decision.

CLAY: Great. Great.

LULA: And everyone will pretend they don't know your name, and then . . . [*She pauses heavily.*] later, when they have to, they'll claim a friendship that denies your sterling character.

CLAY [*Kissing her neck and fingers*]: And then what?

LULA: Then? Well then we'll go down the street, late night, eating apples and winding very deliberately toward my house.

CLAY: Deliberately?

LULA: I mean, we'll look in all the shop windows, and make fun of the queers. Maybe we'll meet a Jewish Buddhist and flatten his conceits over some very pretentious coffee.

CLAY: In honor of whose God?

LULA: Mine.

CLAY: Who is . . . ?

LULA: Me . . . and you?

CLAY: A corporate godhead.

LULA: Exactly. Exactly. [*Notices one of the other people entering.*]

CLAY: Go on with the chronicle. Then what happens to us?

LULA [*A mild depression, but she still makes her description *triumphant and increasingly direct*]:   To my house, of course.

CLAY: Of course.

LULA: And up the narrow steps of the tenement.

CLAY: You live in a tenement?

LULA: Wouldn't live anywhere else. Reminds me specifically of my novel form of insanity.

CLAY: Up the tenement stairs.

LULA: And with my apple-eating hand I push open the door, and lead you, my tender big-eyed prey, into my—God, what can I call it—into my hovel.

CLAY: Then what happens?

LULA: After the dancing and games, after the long drinks and long walks, the real fun begins.

CLAY: Ah, the real fun. [*Embarrassed, in spite of himself.*] Which is . . . ?

LULA [*Laughs at him*]:   Real fun in the dark house. Hah! Real fun in the dark house, high up above the street and the ignorant cowboys. I lead you in, holding your wet hand gently in my hand. . . .

CLAY: Which is not wet?

LULA: Which is dry as ashes.

CLAY: And cold?

LULA: Don't think you'll get out of your responsibility that way. It's not cold at all. You Fascist! Into my dark living room. Where we'll sit and talk endlessly, endlessly.

CLAY: About what?

LULA: About what? About your manhood, what do you think? What do you think we've been talking about all this time?

CLAY: Well, I didn't know it was that. That's for sure. Every other thing in the world but that. [*Notices another person entering, looks quickly, almost involuntarily up and down the car, seeing the other people in the car.*] Hey, I didn't even notice when those people got on.

LULA: Yeh, I know.

CLAY: Man, this subway is slow.

LULA: Yeh, I know.

CLAY: Well, go on. We were talking about my manhood.

LULA: We still are. All the time.

CLAY: We were in your living room.

LULA: My dark living room. Talking endlessly.

CLAY: About my manhood.

LULA: I'll make you a map of it. Just as soon as we get to my house.

CLAY: Well, that's great.

LULA: One of the things we do while we talk. And screw.

CLAY [*Trying to make his smile broader and less shaky*]:   We finally got there.

LULA: And you'll call my rooms black as a grave. You'll say, "This place is like Juliet's tomb."

CLAY [*Laughs*]:   I might.

LULA: I know. You've probably said it before.

CLAY: And is that all? The whole grand tour?

LULA: Not all. You'll say to me very close to my face, many, many times, you'll say, even whisper, that you love me.

CLAY: Maybe I will.

LULA: And you'll be lying.

CLAY: I wouldn't lie about something like that.

LULA: Hah. It's the only kind of thing you will lie about. Especially if you think it'll keep me alive.

CLAY: Keep you alive? I don't understand.

LULA [*Bursting out laughing, but too shrilly*]:   Don't understand? Well, don't look at me. It's the path I take, that's all. Where both feet take me when I set them down. One in front of the other.

CLAY: Morbid. Morbid. You sure you're not an actress? All that self-aggrandizement.

LULA: Well, I told you I wasn't an actress . . . but I also told you I lie all the time. Draw your own conclusions.

CLAY: I will. And is this all of our life together you've described? There's no more?

LULA: I've told you all I know. Or almost all.

CLAY: There're no funny parts?

LULA: I thought it was all funny.

CLAY: But you mean peculiar, not hah, hah.

LULA: You don't know what I mean.

CLAY: Well, tell me the almost part then. You said almost all. What else? I want the whole story.

LULA [*Searching aimlessly through her bag. She begins to talk breathlessly, with a light and silly tone*]:   All stories are whole stories. All of 'em. Our whole story . . . nothing but change. How could things go on like that forever? Huh? [*Slaps him on the shoulder, begins finding things in her bag, taking them out and throwing them over her shoulder into the aisle.*] Except, I do go on as I do. Apples and long walks with deathless, intelligent lovers. But you mix it up. Look out the window, all the time. Turning pages. Change change change. Till, shit, I don't know you. Wouldn't, for that matter. You're too serious. I bet you're even too serious to be psychoanalyzed. Like all those Jewish poets from Yonkers, who leave their mothers looking for other mothers, or others' mothers, on whose baggy tits they lay their fumbling heads. Their poems are always funny, and all about sex.

CLAY: They sound great. Like movies.

LULA: But you change. [*Blankly.*] And things work on you till you hate them.

[*More people come into the train. They come closer to the couple, some of them not sitting, but swinging drearily on the straps, staring at the two with uncertain interest.*]

CLAY: Wow. All these people, so suddenly. They must all come from the same place.

LULA: Right. That they do.

CLAY: Oh? You know about them, too?

LULA: Oh, yeh. About them more than I know about you. Do they frighten you?

CLAY: Frighten me? Why should they frighten me?

LULA: Cause you're an escaped nigger.

CLAY: Yeh?

LULA: Cause you crawled through the wire, and made tracks
to my side.

CLAY: Wire?

LULA: Don't they have wire around plantations?

CLAY: You must be Jewish. All you can think about is wire.
Plantations didn't have any wire. Plantations were big, open,
whitewashed places like heaven, and everybody on 'em was
grooved to be there. Just strumming and hummin' all day.

LULA: Yes, yes.

CLAY: And that's how the blues was born.

LULA: Yes, yes. And that's how the blues was born. [*Begins
to make up a song that becomes quickly hysterical. As she
sings she rises from her seat still throwing things out of her
bag into the aisle, beginning a rhythmical shudder and twist-
like wiggle, which she continues up and down the aisle, bump-
ing into many of the standing people and tripping over the
feet of those sitting. Each time she runs into a person, she
lets out a very vicious piece of profanity, wiggling and step-
ping all the time.*] And that's how the blues was born. Yes.
Yes. Son of a bitch, get out of the way. Yes. Quack. Yes. Yea.
And that's how the blues was born. Ten little niggers sitting
on a limb, but none of them ever looked like him. [*Points to
CLAY, returns toward the seat, with her hands extended for
him to rise and dance with her.*] And that's how blues was
born. Yes. Come on, Clay. Let's do the Nasty. Rub bellies.
Rub bellies.

CLAY [*Waves his hands to refuse. He is embarrassed, but deter-
mined to get a kick out of the proceedings*]:   Hey, what
was in those apples? Mirror, mirror on the wall, who's the
fairest one of all? Snow White, baby, and don't you forget it.

LULA [*Grabbing for his hands, which he draws away*]:   Come
on, Clay. Let's rub bellies on the train. The Nasty. The Nasty.
Do the gritty grind, like our ol' rag-head mammy. Grind till
you lose your mind. Shake it, shake it, shake it, shake it!

OOOOweeee! Come on, Clay. Let's do the choo choo train shuffle, the navel scratcher.

CLAY: Hey, you coming on like the lady who smoked up her grass skirt.

LULA [*Becoming annoyed that he will not dance, and becoming more animated as if to embarrass him still further*]: Come on, Clay . . . let's do the thing. Uhh! Uhh! Clay! Clay! You middle-class black bastard. Forget your social-working mother for a few seconds and let's knock stomachs. Clay, you liver-lipped white man. You would-be Christian. You ain't no nigger, you're just a dirty white man. Get up, Clay. Dance with me, Clay.

CLAY: Lula! Sit down, now. Be cool.

LULA [*Mocking him, in wild dance*]: "Be cool. Be cool." That's all you know . . . shaking that wildroot creme oil on your knotty head, jackets buttoning up to your chin, so full of white man's words. Christ. God. Get up and scream at these people. A dada man. Like scream meaningless shit in these hopeless faces. [*She screams at people in train, still dancing.*] Red trains cough Jewish underwear for keeps! Expanding smells of silence. Gravy snot whistling like sea birds. Clay. Clay, you got to break out. Don't sit there dying the way they want you to die. Get up.

CLAY: Oh, sit down. [*He moves to restrain her.*] Sit down, goddamn it.

LULA [*Twisting out of his reach*]: Screw yourself, Uncle Tom. Thomas Wooly-Head. [*Begins to dance a kind of jig, mocking CLAY with loud forced humor.*] There is Uncle Tom . . . I mean, Uncle Thomas Wooly-Head. With old white matted mane. He hobbles on his wooden cane. Old Tom. Old Tom. Let the white man hump his ol' mama, and he jes' shuffle off in the woods and hide his gentle gray head. Ol' Thomas Wooly-Head.

[*Some of the other riders are laughing now. A drunk gets up and joins LULA in her dance, singing as best he can, her*] "song." CLAY *gets up out of his seat, and visibly scans the faces of the other riders.*]

CLAY: Lula! Lula! [*She is dancing and turning, still shouting as loud as she can. The drunk too is shouting, and waving his hands wildly.*] Lula . . . you dumb bitch. Why don't you stop it? [*He rushes half stumbling from his seat, and grabs one of her flailing arms.*]

LULA: Let me go! You black son-of-a-bitch. [*She struggles against him.*] Let me go! Help!

[CLAY *is dragging her towards her seat, and the drunk seeks to interfere. He grabs* CLAY *around the shoulders and begins wrestling with him.* CLAY *clubs the drunk to the floor without releasing* LULA, *who is still screaming.* CLAY *finally gets her to the seat and throws her into it.*]

CLAY: Now, you shut the hell up. [*Grabbing her shoulders.*] Just shut up. You don't know what you're talking about. You don't know anything. So just keep your stupid mouth closed.

LULA: You're afraid of white people. And your father was. Uncle Tom Big Lip!

CLAY [*Slaps her as hard as he can, across the mouth.* LULA's *head bangs against the back of the seat. When she raises it again,* CLAY *slaps her again*]:   Now, you shut up and let me talk. [*He turns toward the other riders, some of whom are sitting on the edge of their seats. The drunk is on one knee, rubbing his head, and singing softly the same song. He shuts up, too, when he sees* CLAY *watching him. The others go back to newspapers, or stare out the windows.*] Shit, you don't have any sense, Lula, nor feelings either. I could murder you now. Such a tiny ugly throat. I could squeeze it flat, and watch you turn blue, on a humble. For dull kicks. And all these weak-faced ofays squatting around here, staring over their papers at me. Murder them too. Even if they expected it. That man there . . . [*Points to a well-dressed man.*] I could rip that *Times* right out of his hand, as skinny, and middle-classed as I am, I could rip that paper out of his hand and just as easily rip out his throat. It takes no great effort. For what? To kill you soft idiots? You don't understand anything but luxury.

LULA: You fool!

CLAY [*Pushing her against the seat*]: I'm not telling you again Tallulah Bankhead! Luxury. In your face and your fingers. You telling me what I ought to do. [*Sudden scream frightening the whole coach.*] Well, don't! Don't you tell me anything! If I'm a middle-class fake white man . . . let me be. And let me be in the way I want. [*Through his teeth.*] I'll rip your lousy breasts off! Let me be who I feel like being. Uncle Tom. Thomas. Whoever. It's none of your business. You don't know anything except what's there for you to see. An act. Lies. Device. Not the pure heart, the pumping black heart. You don't ever know that. And I sit here, in this buttoned-up suit to keep myself from cutting all your throats. I mean wantonly. You great liberated whore! You fuck some black man, and right away you're an expert on black people. What a lotta shit that is. The only thing you know is that you come if he bangs you hard enough. And that's all. The belly rub? You wanted to do the belly rub? Shit, you don't even know how. You don't know how. That ol' dipty-dip shit you do, rolling your ass like an elephant. That's not my kind of belly rub. Belly rub is not Queens. Belly rub is dark places, with big hats and overcoats held up with one arm. Belly rub hates you. Old baldheaded four-eyed ofays popping their fingers . . . and don't know yet what they're doing. They say, "I love Bessie Smith." And don't even understand that Bessie Smith is saying, "Kiss my ass, kiss my black unruly ass." Before love, suffering, desire, anything you can explain, she's saying, and very plainly, "Kiss my black ass." And if you don't know that, it's you that's doing the kissing.

Charlie Parker? Charlie Parker. All the hip white boys scream for Bird. And Bird saying, "Up your ass, feebleminded ofay! Up your ass." And they sit there talking about the tortured genius of Charlie Parker. Bird would've played not a note of music if he just walked up to East Sixty-seventh Street

and killed the first ten white people he saw. Not a note! And
I'm the great would-be poet. Yes. That's right! Poet. Some
kind of bastard literature . . . all it needs is a simple knife
thrust. Just let me bleed you, you loud whore, and one poem
vanished. A whole people of neurotics, struggling to keep
from being sane. And the only thing that would cure the
neurosis would be your murder. Simple as that. I mean, if I
murdered you, then other white people would begin to understand me. You understand? No. I guess not. If Bessie Smith
had killed some white people, she wouldn't have needed that
music. She could have talked very straight and plain about
the world. No metaphors. No grunts. No wiggles in the dark
of her soul. Just straight two and two are four. Money. Power.
Luxury. Like that. All of them. Crazy niggers turning their
backs on sanity. When all it needs is that simple act. Murder.
Just murder! Would make us all sane. [*Suddenly weary.*]

   Ahhh. Shit. But who needs it? I'd rather be a fool. Insane.
Safe with my words, and no deaths, and clean, hard thoughts,
urging me to new conquests. My people's madness. Hah!
That's a laugh. My people. They don't need me to claim
them. They got legs and arms of their own. Personal in-
sanities. Mirrors. They don't need all these words. They don't
need any defense. But listen, though, one more thing. And
you tell this to your father, who's probably the kind of man
who needs to know at once. So he can plan ahead. Tell him
not to preach so much rationalism and cold logic to these niggers. Let them alone. Let them sing curses at you in code and
see your filth as simple lack of style. Don't make the mistake
through some irresponsible surge of Christian charity, of talking too much about the advantages of Western rationalism,
or the great intellectual legacy of the white man, or maybe
they'll begin to listen. And then, maybe one day, you'll find
they actually do understand exactly what you are talking
about, all these fantasy people. All these blues people. And
on that day, as sure as shit, when you really believe you can
"accept" them into your fold, as half-white trusties late of

the subject peoples, with no more blues, except the very old ones, and not a watermelon in sight, the great missionary heart will have triumphed, and all of those ex-coons will be stand-up Western men, with eyes for clean, hard, useful lives, sober, pious and sane, and they'll murder you. They'll murder you, and have very rational explanations. Very much like your own. They'll cut your throats, and drag you out to the edge of your cities so the flesh can fall away from your bones in sanitary isolation.

LULA [*Her voice takes on a different, more businesslike quality*]: I've heard enough.

CLAY [*Reaching for his books*]:   I bet you have. I guess I better collect my stuff and get off this train. Looks like we won't be acting out that little pageant you outlined before.

LULA: No. We won't. You're right about that, at least. [*She turns to look quickly around the rest of the car.*] All right!
[*The others respond.*]

CLAY [*Bending across the girl to retrieve his belongings*]: Sorry, baby, I don't think we could make it.
[*As he is bending over her, the girl brings up a small knife and plunges it into* CLAY's *chest. Twice. He slumps across her knees, his mouth working stupidly.*]

LULA: Sorry is right. [*Turning to the others in the car who have already gotten up from their seats.*] Sorry is the rightest thing you've said. Get this man off me! Hurry, now! [*The others come and drag* CLAY's *body down the aisle.*] Throw his body off between the cars—and the rest of you get off at the next stop.
[LULA *busies herself straightening her things. Getting everything in order, she takes out a notebook and makes quick scribbling notes. Drops notebook into her bag. The train apparently stops and the others get off, leaving her alone in the coach.*

Very soon a young Negro of about 20 comes into the coach with a couple of books under his arm. He sits a few seats in back of* LULA. *She starts to move out of the car, sees the* *young man, changes her mind, and sits somewhat nearer to him. When she is seated she turns and gives him a long slow look. She smiles. He becomes aware of her staring and looks up from his book. He drops the book to his lap as they continue to stare at one another. She turns away, satisfied that he is intrigued, takes an apple from her bag. She bites into it, smiling, as the lights and sound slowly fade.*]

CURTAIN